P9-EJJ-340

WITHDRAWN

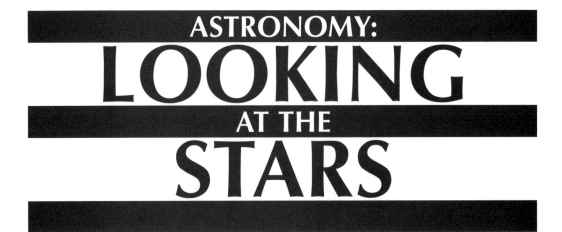

ASTRONOMY: LOOKING AT THE STARS

Inside the illustration:

DIALOGO
di
GALILEO GALILEI LINCEO
Al SER.^{mo} FERD. II. GRAN. DVCA DI
TOSC ANA

Stefano Della Bella F.

This imaginary discussion between three great astronomers—(from left to right) Aristotle, Ptolemy, and Copernicus—illustrates the way that early thinkers living centuries apart built upon one another's work to develop the science of astronomy.

INNOVATORS

ASTRONOMY:
LOOKING
AT THE
STARS

CONTRA COSTA COUNTY LIBRARY

Susan and Steven Wills

The Oliver Press, Inc.
Minneapolis

3 1901 03106 2922

This book is dedicated to Ma Mere, the brightest star in our sky.

Copyright © 2001 by The Oliver Press, Inc.

All rights reserved.
No part of this book may be reproduced in any form or by
any means without permission in writing from the publisher.
Please address inquiries to:

The Oliver Press, Inc.
Charlotte Square
5707 West 36th Street
Minneapolis, MN 55416-2510

Library of Congress Cataloging-in-Publication Data
Wills, Susan.
Astronomy: looking at the stars / Susan and Steven Wills.
p. cm. — (Innovators ; 9)
Includes bibliographical references and index.
    Summary: Profiles seven thinkers who developed the science
of astronomy: Claudius Ptolemy, Nicolaus Copernicus,
Tycho Brahe, Johannes Kepler, Galileo Galilei, Isaac Newton,
and William Herschel.
ISBN 1-881508-76-5 (library binding)
1. Astronomers—Biography—Juvenile literature. 2. Astronomy—
History—Juvenile literature. [1. Astronomers. 2. Astronomy—
History.] I. Wills, Steven R. II. Title. III. Series.

QB35.W63 2000
520'.92'2—dc21
[B]   00-052856
                                    CIP
                                    AC

ISBN 1-881508-76-5
Printed in the United States of America
07 06 05 04 03 02 01   8 7 6 5 4 3 2 1

CONTENTS

The Birth of a Science

Astronomy may be the oldest science. Precisely how old is difficult to say, since it is impossible to know when the first watchers looked up into the dome of countless stars and wondered at the incredible sights there. One thing is clear, however: the basic practice of astronomy had been well established by the time humans formed the first civilizations.

Since the beginning of human history, people from nearly every culture have gazed into the sky and invented stories to make sense of what they observed. Ancient Egyptians, for example, saw the Sun rise in the east, move across the sky in the day, set in the west, and then appear in the east again at daybreak. They also noted that the sky looked blue, like a great body of water overhead. Their conclusion was that the Sun god, Ra, sailed from east to west each day in a boat of fire. He then disappeared into the underworld until the next morning.

The science of astronomy is based on one of humanity's oldest fantasies: reaching beyond the boundaries of the Earth to probe the mysterious space beyond.

The oldest evidence of astronomy as a science is a calendar carved onto a piece of bone found near the Congo River in Africa, dating back to 6500 B.C. By 3000 B.C., the Egyptians had developed a 365-day calendar, and about 1500 years later they invented the sundial, which measured the time of day by the angle of the Sun.

celestial: relating to the sky or the heavens

It is likely that even the earliest nomadic peoples used the patterns of the Sun, Moon, stars, and planets to navigate as they traveled from place to place in search of food. As humans formed stable civilizations, however, measuring time became the most practical use that ancient sky watchers could make of their observations. The world's earliest known villages based on farming, which formed in Mesopotamia around 7000 B.C., could not have grown into successful cities without a knowledge of when to plant, when to expect the rainy season, and when to harvest. The easiest way to tell the time of year is to notice the patterns of the Sun and stars over the course of a long period of time. Which day is the longest day, and which is the shortest? When do the days stop becoming shorter and begin to become longer? Which star patterns are at a particular point in the night sky just before the rainy season begins? To understand the cycles of nature requires a primitive understanding of the relationship between Earth and the Sun . . . in other words, astronomy.

Astronomy (from the Greek *astro*, meaning "star," and *nomos*, meaning "system of law") is the science that studies the stars, planets, and all other celestial bodies. It is concerned with their origins, evolution, physical conditions, movements, distances, and the forces that tie them together. Although astronomy began as simply a means of telling time and location, it soon developed into a full-fledged area of study, characterized by patient observation and detailed record-keeping. As early as 2500 B.C. in

what is now England, work began on Stonehenge, a group of standing stones that are thought to have been aligned to track the movements of the Sun and Moon and to measure eclipses. Around 1300 B.C., Chinese astronomers embarked on a long, precise study of eclipses, recording 900 solar eclipses and 600 lunar eclipses over the next 2,600 years. In about 700 B.C., the Babylonians went one step further by studying their own astronomical records and finding patterns in the appearances of lunar eclipses that helped them to predict when future ones would occur.

Stonehenge's four rings of stones are aligned with the positions of the Sun at the longest and shortest days of the year.

eclipse: the passage of one celestial body through the shadow of another. In a **solar eclipse**, the Moon blocks the light from the Sun to Earth; in a **lunar eclipse**, Earth blocks the light of the Sun to the Moon.

Anaxagoras was the teacher of some of the most famous men of his time, including the politician Pericles, the playwright Euripedes, and the philosopher Socrates. Despite his prestige, he was eventually banished from Athens for his beliefs, including the idea that the Moon is made of rock and reflects the Sun's rays.

Milky Way: a softly glowing band of light visible in the night sky from Earth, produced by the stars that make up the galaxy in which Earth and its solar system are located. This galaxy is often called the Milky Way galaxy.

The more deeply these early watchers looked into the canopy of stars, however, the more complex it appeared. It became clear that the myths of the storytellers were not sophisticated enough to explain all the mysteries of the heavens. In the last centuries B.C. in Greece, a few individual thinkers made names for themselves by developing theories about the structure and workings of the universe. Anaxagoras (500-428 B.C.) correctly theorized that the Moon shines by the light it receives from the Sun and that lunar eclipses occur when Earth blocks the Sun's light. Democritus (460-370 B.C.) originated the idea that the Milky Way is not a white cloud but a string of thousands upon thousands of stars. The great philosopher Aristotle (384-322 B.C.) argued that the circular shadow seen on the Moon during a lunar eclipse was proof that Earth is a sphere, and Eratosthenes (276-194 B.C.) used geometry to calculate Earth's circumference to within a few percent of its actual size.

Another early watcher who set the stage for the first real scientific investigation of astronomy was a Greek mathematician, Aristarchus of Samos (310-230 B.C.). By 270 B.C., he had developed a way to calculate the diameters of the Sun and Moon and their distances from Earth. Although his results were inaccurate, he realized that the Sun was much larger than Earth. From this, he concluded (contrary to what most people assumed at the time) that the Sun was the center of the universe. Aristarchus had correctly described our solar system, but his theory was not accepted during his life—or for 1,800 years to come.

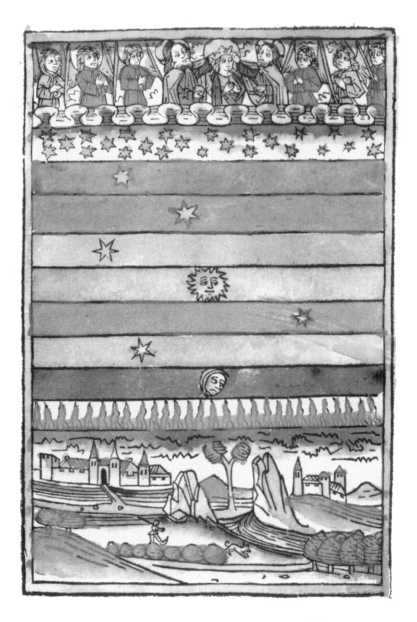

Despite Aristarchus's breakthroughs, the Earth-centered view of the universe persisted for nearly another 2,000 years. This 1481 engraving shows the Moon, Sun, planets, and stars arranged in layers over the Earth, with a Christian image of Heaven occupying the outermost reaches of space.

It would take the work of many other minds over the course of the following centuries to create and then to prove an accurate view of the universe, and scientists today are still wrestling with its secrets. As is often the case in the growth of science, the more information is gathered, the more questions there are to be investigated.

Astronomers have developed complex instruments to help them observe the skies more fully and accurately. Here, the Danish astronomer Ole Römer (1644-1710) is shown using his innovative transit telescope, which he built in the 1680s to measure more precisely the position of stars as they cross ("transit") a certain point over the Earth.

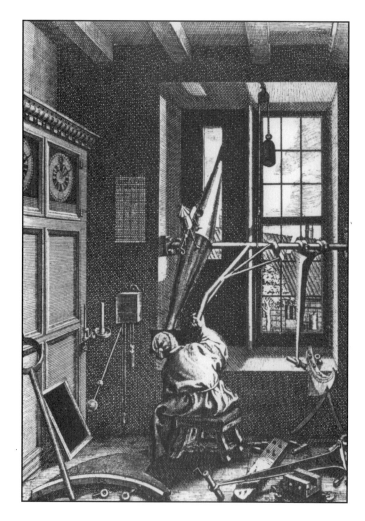

In its early forms, astronomy was barely distinct from other subjects—philosophy, mathematics, astrology, and religion. But gradually, a series of scientists established astronomy as a unique discipline, complete with its own instruments, methods, and revolutionary discoveries. In this book, we will follow the growth of astronomy by looking over the shoulders of those who worked to organize and develop it. Some—like Tycho Brahe, Galileo Galilei, and William Herschel—invented and improved tools to conduct systematic studies of the skies, discovering never-before-seen phenomena and gathering valuable data about the nature and movements of the heavens. Others—including Claudius Ptolemy, Nicolaus Copernicus, Johannes Kepler, and Isaac Newton—used such observations to make mathematical calculations, discover physical laws, and devise brilliant new theories that described the structure of the universe itself.

Each of these scientists stood on what was known at the time and reached for something higher, adding another step for the next to stand on. The ladder of their accomplishments led to the development of astronomy as a science. It would not be an easy path, and not every step would lead forward, but the direction of the climb—toward discovery and understanding—was never in doubt.

astrology: the study of the positions of the Sun, Moon, stars, and planets in the belief that they influence earthly events and human fortunes

CHAPTER ONE

Claudius Ptolemy and the Rhythm of the Spheres

What if the Sun were not at the center of the solar system? What if it were actually our Earth at the center? What would change for us? If we walked outside in the day or the night, how would things appear different?

The truth is, we wouldn't be able to see any difference. In fact, the whole idea of Earth moving around the Sun doesn't seem as logical as the Sun moving around the Earth. After all, don't we see the Sun move across the sky each day? And it certainly doesn't feel as if we're hurtling through space.

For early watchers of the skies, a universe with the Earth spinning around the Sun seemed to contradict all the observable evidence, not to mention common sense. Claudius Ptolemy (TALL-uh-mee), the first astronomer to push the study of the heavens out of the realm of philosophy and into the realm of science, was no different. But although his assumptions were fundamentally incorrect, he used them

There are no existing portraits of Claudius Ptolemy that were made during his lifetime in the second century A.D. (This engraving was created in the 1400s and thus shows him in medieval dress.) But although his image did not survive, Ptolemy's work influenced the science of astronomy for centuries to come.

as the basis of a remarkable series of achievements. In the course of his career, Ptolemy managed to gather a comprehensive catalog of the stars; calculate tables to predict the movements of the Sun, Moon, and planets; create a means of drawing maps that minimized distortion; and give physical form to a theory of the universe that would dominate Western thought for the next 1,400 years.

The known facts of Ptolemy's personal life are few, but we can still get an idea of who he was from the age in which he lived. He was born sometime around A.D. 100, when the Roman Empire was at its height in both power and size. Ptolemy was of Greek or Egyptian descent and lived in Alexandria, a

In this 1808 German engraving, Ptolemy (third from left) is rewarded for his scholarly achievements by his colleagues in the library at Alexandria.

city on the Mediterranean coast of Egypt that served as a prime base of the Roman Empire in northern Africa at the time. He worked in the city's legendary library, where in 10 research halls—each devoted to a separate subject—were stored an estimated 400,000 books and scrolls. Ptolemy's scientific education was enriched not only by the community of scholars that gathered there, but also by his free access to the world's greatest collection of written knowledge.

In Ptolemy's time, scholarship centered on the philosophy of the ancient Greeks. Plato (427-348 B.C.), the most highly regarded of these early philosophers, had little interest in practical astronomy. Instead, he sought the spiritual essence of things, presenting theories of how he believed the universe ought to work. Plato thought that because the universe must certainly be perfect, the celestial bodies and their orbits must resemble the most perfect of shapes—the circle. He reasoned that since humanity was the most important part of creation, Earth must be the center of the universe. Thus, Plato envisioned the spherical Earth encased in a series of progressively larger spheres that formed the universe. The sphere nearest Earth held the Moon in its place, the next six held the planets and the Sun, and the outermost sphere contained all the stars. Nested within one another like hollow balls, these spheres spun around the Earth, carrying all the celestial bodies with them at a regular speed. Although close observation would prove that the planets do not move at a constant speed and their orbits are not perfectly circular, Plato said simply,

Plato was a student of the great philosopher Socrates (469-399 B.C.). Socrates, in turn, had been taught by Anaxagoras (500-428 B.C.), one of the earliest Greek thinkers to develop scientific theories about the heavens.

orbit: the movement of one celestial body around another, under the influence of gravitational force

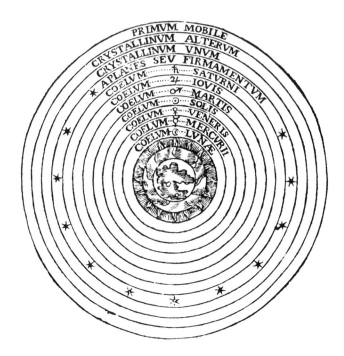

A basic diagram of the Earth-centered universe that was envisioned by Plato and developed by Aristotle. In the middle are the four elements—the earth and water that make up the planet Earth, the air that composes the atmosphere, and the fire that was thought to lie beyond. These are surrounded by spheres for the Moon, Mercury, Venus, the Sun, Mars, Jupiter, Saturn, and the stars.

"The movements [of the planets] can be comprehended only by reason and thought, not by sight." Clearly, astronomy was not yet a science, but a branch of philosophy in which ideas were more important than hard data.

Plato's vision of the universe was meant only as a convenient way of looking at things, not a physical reality. His pupil Aristotle (384-322 B.C.), however, believed that the goal of science was to recognize in the real world the spiritual essence that Plato had written about. The spheres had to be solid objects, he thought, perhaps made out of crystal. They had to move within each other around the Earth, which must be at rest in the center. By the time he was done designing his universe, Aristotle needed no less than 55 of these spheres to account for all the visible movements of objects in space. But he remained firm in his belief that although Earth was imperfect and always changing, the heavens were flawless and permanent, and the structure of the universe must follow these characteristics. By Ptolemy's time, the Earth-centered spheres of Aristotle and Plato were accepted as truth, and this incorrect "truth" was to haunt Ptolemy—as it would other astronomers for hundreds of years to come.

If the main source of Ptolemy's thinking came from Plato and Aristotle, his main source of data about the universe can be traced to the Greek astronomer Hipparchus (180-127 B.C.). Much more scientific in his approach than Aristotle, during the course of his career Hipparchus compiled a detailed catalog of 850 stars and discovered an effect known as the precession of the equinoxes. Hipparchus viewed Earth as the center of the universe and believed the stars revolved on a crystal sphere, but he used a massive collection of observations to give his theories credibility. In fact, Hipparchus had realized that Aristotle's vision of the universe was too simple and set out to improve it. Rather than collecting observations and then forming a conclusion from the facts, however, he began with the basic theories of Aristotle and tried to tinker with the system until his observations matched the theory.

Hipparchus was Ptolemy's hero. But Ptolemy realized that Hipparchus had failed to match his observations of planetary motions with his Earth-centered theory. It became Ptolemy's goal to "save

Aristotle thought that the heavenly spheres were made out of an unknown fifth element, or "quintessence." They are commonly referred to, however, as "crystal" spheres because they were thought to be solid and transparent like glass.

---

precession of the equinoxes: the 25,800-year cycle in which the equinox (the time when the Sun crosses the space above the equator) occurs slightly earlier each year, due to the slow wobbling of Earth on its axis

---

To create his model of the motions of celestial bodies, Hipparchus compared the astronomical records of the ancient Babylonians with his own observations, made on the Greek island of Rhodes between 141 and 127 B.C.

The object which the astronomer must strive to achieve is this: to demonstrate that all the phenomena in the sky are produced by uniform and circular motions.
—Ptolemy

the appearances" by finding a way to fit actual observations of the movements of the planets into Aristotle's model. He would correct Hipparchus's flaws. Along the way, Ptolemy would see his world as few thinkers ever had. His desire to match data with theory would lead to the creation of the world's first enduring and truly scientific astronomical work.

THE BREAKTHROUGH

Between A.D. 145 and 150, Ptolemy produced a complete reference to the astronomy of his time in a collection of 13 volumes that came to be known as the *Almagest*. In it, Ptolemy summarized basic astronomical theory as he knew it—the motions of the Sun, the Moon, the five known planets (Mercury, Venus, Mars, Jupiter, and Saturn), and the stars, as well as events such as eclipses. But Ptolemy did more than simply assemble existing knowledge. He showed, for perhaps the first time in history, how to convert astronomical observations into mathematical formulas that could be used to calculate the positions of the Sun, Moon, and planets for any given time in the present or future. He then applied these formulas to create a working model of the universe.

The first and second volumes of the *Almagest* described the basics of Ptolemy's view of the universe. An Earth that never moved was located in the center of a sphere covered with fixed stars, which made one complete revolution around the Earth from east to west every 24 hours. As it moved, this outer sphere carried along with it the smaller interior spheres of the Sun, Moon, and planets, causing those bodies to orbit Earth. Ptolemy then described the mathematics that supported this theory.

The third book of the *Almagest* dealt with the movements of the Sun, which dictate the length of the year and the seasons. At this point, Ptolemy's theories became problematic. According to Aristotle and Hipparchus, the Sun was supposed to revolve

Ptolemy titled his work *Megale Mathematike Syntaxis* (*Great Mathematical Compilation*), but after being translated into Arabic in A.D. 827 it became known as *Almagest*—from the Arabic word for "the greatest."

equinox: either of the two times of the year—in spring and autumn—when the Sun crosses the celestial equator (the space above Earth's equator), making day and night of equal length in all parts of the Earth.

solstice: either of the two times of the year—in summer and winter—when the Sun is farthest away from the celestial equator. In the Northern Hemisphere, the summer solstice is the longest day of the year and the winter solstice is the shortest.

magnitude: a measure of the brightness of a star or other celestial object, expressed on a scale in which the lowest numbers indicate the greatest brightness

ellipse: an oval-shaped figure with two centers of symmetry, called **foci** (plural of focus). The orbits of planets are elliptical.

around Earth at an even speed, yet observations showed that this was not true. For example, the time from the spring equinox until the summer solstice was found to be one day longer than from the summer solstice to the fall equinox, although these two time periods should theoretically have been identical. To keep his calculations consistent with Hipparchus's, Ptolemy used an incorrect date for the spring equinox. This manipulation of the numbers would affect all his other data.

Books four and five of the *Almagest* involved the motion of the Moon. The sixth book dealt with solar and lunar eclipses, setting up the formulas for predicting eclipse dates and durations. With his pioneering methods, Ptolemy was even able to calculate eclipses for different geographical locations—an especially useful feature, considering the vast territory that the Roman Empire occupied at that time. Books seven and eight were all about the stars. Most of this work centered on Ptolemy's massive star catalog, which listed 1,022 individual stars and organized them by constellation, latitude, longitude, and magnitude.

The remaining five books of the *Almagest* dealt with the motions of the planets. Here, the problem of "saving appearances" and getting observations to match theory became a real struggle. Although Ptolemy could not have known it at the time, his model would never match the real behavior of the planets. We now know that orbits are not circular but elliptical, and planets do not move at a uniform speed but actually speed up as they approach the Sun.

To approximate this irregular motion, Ptolemy had to add three "techniques" to his model of the universe.

The first technique, the epicycle, was originally created by Apollonius of Perga around 200 B.C. In an epicycle, a planet orbited an imaginary point while that imaginary point orbited Earth. Epicycles were developed to explain why planets—most notably Mars—occasionally seem to move in retrograde, or in reverse. This retrograde motion is now known to be an illusion created by the fact that Earth, the platform from which we observe the movements of the planets, is itself in motion around the Sun. Mars will appear to be moving backward when in fact Earth is moving forward in a smaller, faster orbit and "passing" Mars. Since Ptolemy's model did not include a moving Earth, he used the looping motion of epicycles to create a similar effect.

To understand retrograde motion, imagine the solar system as a racetrack. The planets are like cars moving at different speeds in different lanes. If you are in a car on the inside track (Earth) and you pass a slower car that is driving on an outside track (Mars), from your point of view that car would appear to be moving backwards.

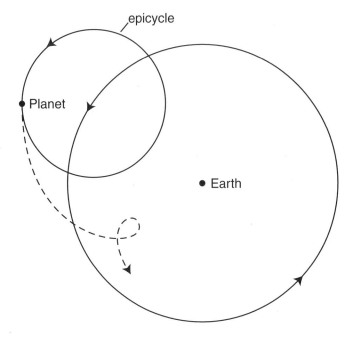

In Ptolemy's theory, a planet moved around in the small circle of the epicycle, while the center of the epicycle moved in a larger circle around Earth. The planet's path (shown as a dotted line) would make small loops as the epicycle orbited, so that at certain times the planet would appear to be moving in retrograde.

The second technique, borrowed from Hipparchus, was the eccentric, which altered the path of a planet so that Earth was slightly off from the center of that planet's orbit. Although it violated the idea that Earth was at the center of the universe, Ptolemy saw his use of the eccentric as only a minor "correction" that was necessary to explain why planets change their speeds and their distances from Earth as they orbit.

When Ptolemy found that these two techniques were not enough to explain the movements of the planets, he created a third strategy called the equant. If, as the eccentric technique assumed, Earth

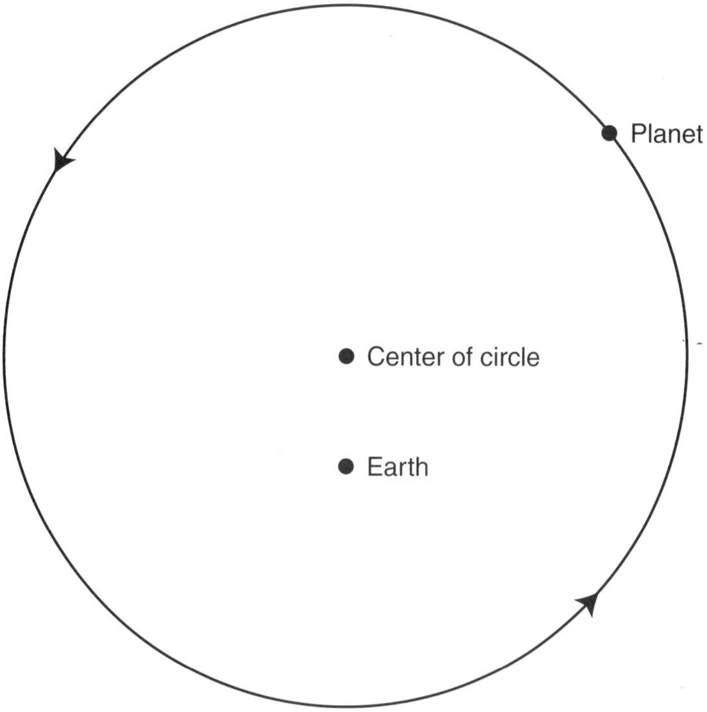

In Ptolemy's eccentric, a planet moved with uniform speed around the center of its orbit, but Earth was not at the center. To observers on Earth, the planet would appear closer and move faster when it was at the bottom of the circle, and more distant and slower when it was at the top.

● Planet

● Center of circle

● Earth

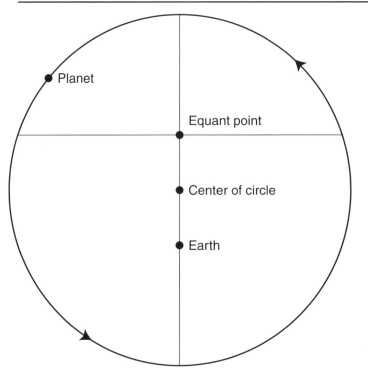

To appear to be moving at a uniform speed to an imaginary observer at the equant point, a planet would have to move slowly at the top of the circle (where the quadrants are smallest) and quickly at the bottom.

was not exactly at the center of an orbital circle, then Ptolemy suggested the idea of an imaginary point located as far from the center of the circle as Earth was, but on the opposite side. This "mirror image" point was the equant. Ptolemy divided a planet's orbital circle into quarters from the point of the equant, and then theorized that the orbiting planet would travel each quadrant in equal time. To do so, the planet would need to vary its speed, since the quadrants were of different sizes. From the point of view of the equant, however, the planet's motion would appear uniform. Use of the equant, along with the epicycle and the eccentric, finally allowed the orbits of the planets to match observational data.

THE RESULT

Although Ptolemy's model finally worked, it did not work perfectly; in fact, it violated the ideas of Aristotle. The use of the eccentric and the epicycle pushed Earth from the exact center of the universe. More importantly, the use of the equant meant that planets did not move in perfect circular motion. Ptolemy's universe had become very complicated and suspiciously artificial, but nevertheless, the *Almagest* served as the standard reference in astronomy for the next 1,400 years.

Although the *Almagest* was Ptolemy's best-known work, his ability to organize information and explain difficult concepts led him to publish books about optics, music, geometry, and astrology. Of the most lasting importance was his eight-volume *Geography*. Educated people in Ptolemy's time already realized that Earth was spherical rather than flat, but they were unable to make maps of that spherical world on a flat surface without distortion. Only the very center of a map could be relied upon as accurate—and merchants and sailors needed more than that. Ptolemy described a mathematically accurate way of projecting a round surface onto a plane, then reviewed the maps of the known world and recorded them using his new projection technique.

The result was an atlas of incredible detail. Although Ptolemy's maps still showed some distortion of space at the edges (enough to convince Christopher Columbus in 1492 that the western route from Europe to Asia was much shorter than it

Ptolemy's entire universe (only about 50 million miles in diameter) could easily fit inside what we now know to be the size of Earth's orbit around the Sun. At the time, however, Ptolemy's estimate seemed enormous. People assumed celestial objects were close to Earth and very small; the ancient Greeks Heraclitus and Lucretius thought the Sun was about the size of a shield, and Anaxagoras was banished for suggesting it might be larger than the southern part of Greece!

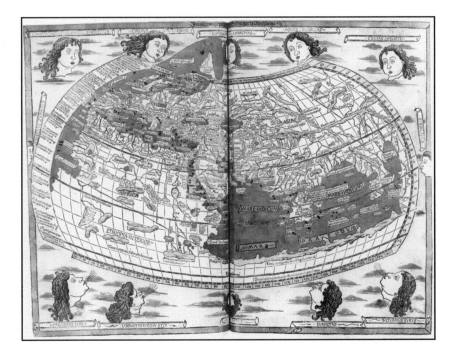

actually is), *Geography* and its map collection endured for centuries to come. Large, highly decorated copies of the book were popular in the mid-fifteenth century, and some of Ptolemy's maps—particularly of Africa—remained in use into the 1800s.

From the standpoint of modern science, it is certainly possible to find errors in Ptolemy's vast quantity of work. The position of the stars does not, as he believed, predict the weather, nor is there an eighth continent at the southern edge of the Indian Ocean, as his maps indicate. Planets do not follow circular orbits, the stars are not fixed on a crystal sphere, and of course the stars and planets do not revolve around Earth. Ptolemy's model of the universe was proven completely wrong by the early

A map of Europe, Africa, and Asia from Ptolemy's Geography

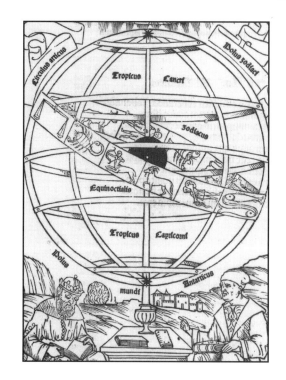

Ptolemy's work remained central to both Islamic and European scholarship for centuries. This 1496 illustration pays tribute to Ptolemy (left) and to Joannes Regiomontanus, who translated the Almagest *for Renaissance readers. The two men sit beneath an armillary sphere, an astronomical tool used to teach the movements of different celestial bodies or to record their locations above Earth.*

eighteenth century, and other aspects of his work began to be criticized. For instance, Ptolemy drew so heavily on the scholarship of others—such as Hipparchus—that it is difficult to know how much of his work is original. Some historians have even accused him of faking or manipulating large portions of his observational data to support his theories; one writer calls him "the most successful fraud in the history of science."

So how can we measure the importance of Claudius Ptolemy? Was he a true scientist or a man trapped by the misguided beliefs of his time? A logical thinker who organized and published the research of others, or a downright phony?

There is no single answer to these questions. Ptolemy was simply one of the last great voices of classical learning before a thousand years of the Dark Ages spread over Europe. In the century after his death, the Roman Empire began to crumble from within. Its political system had become corrupt, and the economy faltered as the gold and silver mines of Spain began to dry up. Plague struck Rome, claiming an average of 2,000 lives per day. Then, with the empire weakened, barbarian tribes rushed in to conquer and destroy the last of Roman civilization and culture. The great library at Alexandria was sacked, and many of the works in it—including the writings of Hipparchus—were lost forever.

Ptolemy's achievement was that he approached science from a different angle than the philosophers of his day. Whereas Aristotle proposed a theory and ignored observable facts, Ptolemy at least tried to make the facts fit the theory. It seems a backward approach, since modern scientists design theories based on the facts. But Ptolemy cannot be judged entirely by modern standards. He admitted that his spheres and epicycles were not supposed to be real machines in the heavens, but merely a means of representing the movement of heavenly bodies. He was most concerned with creating accurate tables of the stars and planets, and in that he was more successful than any other thinker who had come before him. Although Ptolemy's work was later improved upon and then disproved entirely, it still shines as a gift of incredible clarity and knowledge that remains our major source of information about classical astronomy.

CHAPTER TWO

Nicolaus Copernicus and the Sun-Centered Universe

To classical thinkers like Claudius Ptolemy, the idea that Earth stood at the center of the universe seemed natural and logical. Although the Roman civilization began to disintegrate at the end of the fifth century A.D., this geocentric (Earth-centered) theory survived as established fact. The Christian church, which was rising to great social and political power in Europe, accepted geocentrism as being in agreement with descriptions found in the Scriptures. The Bible's book of Genesis, for example, describes God creating Earth and then adding the Sun, Moon, and stars to the sky. It made sense that Earth was the center of creation and that God, the "Prime Mover," caused the heavenly spheres to rotate around it. There was even space in this model for heaven and hell, outside the last sphere of the fixed stars. Supported by established religious beliefs, geocentrism remained unchallenged for centuries.

In an attempt to make Ptolemy's model of the universe more accurate, Nicolaus Copernicus (1473-1543) placed the Sun at the center, revolutionizing the science of astronomy.

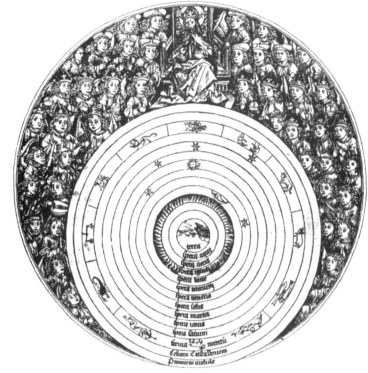

Christianity adapted Ptolemy's theories to portray its own teachings about the order of the universe. In this illustration from the Nuremberg Chronicle, a history of the world published in Germany in 1493, God and the angels occupy the outermost sphere surrounding Earth.

It was not until the 1400s that the fires of Renaissance thinking began to ignite in Europe, waking scientific curiosity from its long sleep. Johannes Gutenberg's invention of the printing press in the 1430s meant that knowledge and literacy could spread far and wide. With information came change that would, in the next hundred years, bring religious rebellion, redraw the political boundaries of nations, and herald a great age of global exploration. Not until the invention of the computer in the twentieth century would a single device change the world as dramatically as Gutenberg's printing press.

This was the world into which Nikolai Kopernik was born on February 19, 1473, in the city of Torun near the Vistula River in northern Poland. Located in a region of dispute between Polish and German kingdoms, Torun was a city rich in both cultures. By most measures, Nikolai Kopernik lived a quiet and unassuming life there. Yet, by the time of his death in 1543, he would shake the certainty with which humanity viewed its place in the heavens. Before that time, astronomy had been little more than a set of philosophical theories. But with Kopernik's breakthrough, the transformation begun 1,400 years earlier by Ptolemy was complete, and astronomy became a science.

Not much is known of Nikolai's childhood. We do know that his father, a merchant, died when Nikolai was 10 years old. The boy was then adopted by his uncle, Lucas Waczenrode, a very wealthy and important clergyman in the Roman Catholic Church in Poland.

Waczenrode helped young Nikolai gain the best education available. Books were spreading all over Europe, and Waczenrode pushed many of them into Nikolai's hands. He also enrolled his adopted son in the best schools in Europe. At the age of 18, Nikolai entered the University of Krakow, where he studied, among other things, mathematics and astronomy. This was followed by studies in the heart of Renaissance Italy: law at the University of Bologna and medicine at the University of Padua.

The word *renaissance*, which means "rebirth," is used to describe the revival of the knowledge of the

By the time Nikolai Kopernik was 30, between six and nine million copies of more than 35,000 different books had already been printed in Europe thanks to Gutenberg's invention of the printing press.

ancient Greeks and Romans that fueled such a great expansion of learning in the fourteenth and fifteenth centuries. Today, the term "Renaissance man" is used to describe someone who has knowledge and skill in many, if not all, of the arts and sciences, and Nikolai Kopernik certainly fit that definition. Throughout his education, he hungrily read Aristotle and Plato, Euclid and Ptolemy, Virgil and Ovid—in short, everything available from classical philosophy, science, and literature. From his study of Plato, Kopernik realized that there must be some simple, underlying structure to the universe. From Aristotle, he learned of the heavens as unchanging layers of transparent spheres, spinning and twisting inside each other as they spun around the Earth. And, of course, from Ptolemy he learned geocentrism.

Kopernik showed an interest in astronomy throughout his education, but investigation of the heavens had to come second to his study of Church law. The ambitions of his uncle seemed to be directing Kopernik's path in life. He received a doctorate in Church law from the University of Ferrara and returned to Poland in 1506 to assist Waczenrode—who was now the Bishop of Ermeland—as a secretary and doctor. Although he kept up his interest in astronomy, observing the night sky whenever he could, he was busy with his uncle's concerns.

After his uncle's death in 1512, Kopernik began full-time work as canon of the cathedral in Frombork, Poland. He was in charge of the cathedral's finances, a position of many benefits and little responsibility. He performed his duties efficiently—even publishing

Kopernik had few friends and never married. Later in life he became romantically involved with his housekeeper, Anna, but he ended the relationship at the bidding of the Church.

a book on money matters—but with his salary assured for life, he now had the luxury to turn his attention to other interests. Kopernik was well educated and talented in many areas of study, but he was also quiet, withdrawn, and unambitious. Who could have known that he was about to upset and redefine humanity's view of the universe?

The cathedral at Frombork

THE BREAKTHROUGH

The broad scope of Kopernik's Renaissance knowledge soon pushed his thoughts beyond the limits of Church doctrine, perhaps first in the area of mathematics. He began to emerge from the shadow of his uncle's career, and, proud of his excellent education, he made the popular move of changing his name to a more classical, "latinized" version—and Nikolai Kopernik became Nicolaus Copernicus.

Copernicus made his first recorded observation of the skies in March 1497, and as early as 1500 he lectured on astronomy to a large audience in Rome.

Although he admired Ptolemy's theories, Copernicus (co-PER-ni-kuss) also recognized their mathematical flaws. By early 1514, he had written *Commentariolus* (*Little Commentary*), a mathematical examination of astronomical theory that was intended to supplement Ptolemy's work, but mainly highlighted the classical astronomer's errors. According to Copernicus, the problem was simple: Ptolemy's theories described the motions of the planets, but his mathematical formulas, when put into practice, did not agree with well-documented observations of planetary motions. As Copernicus later complained, the mathematicians of the Ptolemaic system were "so unsure of the movements of the Sun and Moon that they cannot even explain or observe the constant length of the seasonal year."

Copernicus did not intend to overthrow the Ptolemaic system. He had no doubt that planets moved in circular orbits at uniform speeds. He only sought a more accurate way of "saving the appearances," helping the traditional model of the universe match observational data. To Copernicus, Ptolemy's equant (an imaginary center point around which the planets revolved) was a form of cheating and was far too complicated to exist in nature. Copernicus was looking for the shape and symmetry of the universe itself, the underlying structure—which he called the "principal thing"—that would explain how the heavens moved. After examining the work of Greek philosophers, he decided that the motion of the planets could only be explained satisfactorily if the Sun was at the center of the universe.

In this most beautiful temple [the universe], who would place this lamp [the Sun] in another or better position than that from which it can light up everything at the same time? For the Sun is not inappropriately called by some people the lantern of the universe, its mind by others, and its ruler by still others. . . . And thus the Sun, as if seated on a kingly throne, governs the family of planets that wheel around it.
—Nicolaus Copernicus

Copernicus suggested that the heavenly bodies do not revolve around a single, common center. Although the Moon orbits Earth, Earth and the rest of the planets move around the Sun. He explained the apparent motion of the Sun and stars across the sky as a result of Earth rotating on its axis. He then concluded that the retrograde motion of planets like Mars is an optical illusion also produced by the motion of Earth. Copernicus also assigned the planets a new order, which we now know to be the correct one—Mercury, Venus, Earth, Mars, Jupiter, Saturn. His placement of Mercury and Venus between Earth and the Sun explained why these planets are only visible at dusk or dawn: they cannot be seen at night because the part of Earth facing away from the Sun also faces away from them, while bright daylight makes them impossible to see from the part of Earth that faces the Sun.

retrograde: the brief, regularly occurring, apparently backward movement of a planet in its orbit when seen from Earth

Copernicus's model of the universe

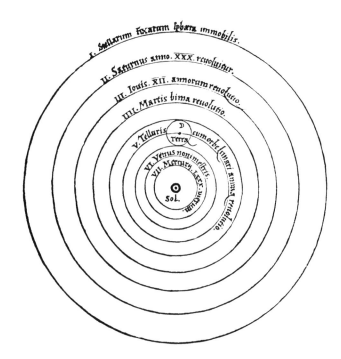

Moving the Sun to the center gave Copernicus a more realistic view of the solar system, allowing him to use geometry to more accurately measure its size and proportions. Based on the apparent distances of Mercury and Venus from the Sun, he was able to locate their positions correctly and determine the relative size of their orbits; then, since the comparative sizes of the other planets' orbits were known, he could calculate their orbital diameters and distances. Copernicus also worked out a detailed formula of the Moon's orbit, from which he was able to set the distance between Earth and the Moon at about 60 times Earth's radius—a figure very close to what is currently used.

But simply taking Earth out of the center and sticking the Sun there was not enough. Copernicus tried to stay true to Aristotle's idea that the unchanging, perfect sphere must be the shape of all things astronomical. Unfortunately, the mathematics of planets orbiting the Sun in perfect spheres proved hardly more accurate in predicting the movements of planets than did Ptolemy's model.

Noticing the inaccuracies of his heliocentric (Sun-centered) model, Copernicus was faced with a choice. He could recognize that, although he was nearing the truth, his model was not yet finished. He could question his own model and consider whether circular orbits were necessary. Or, like Ptolemy, he could "tinker" with his model, adding artificial constructs such as epicycles to try and match the true, observed motions of the planets.

He chose to tinker.

The sphere is the most perfect, the most capacious of figures . . . wherein neither beginning nor end can be found.
—Nicolaus Copernicus

epicycle: in Ptolemaic theory, a circular orbit whose center moves along the circumference of another, larger, circle

Unfortunately, circular orbits were never going to provide an accurate picture of the solar system. In reality, the planets move in ellipses (ovals), not circles, and his insistence on staying with Aristotle's "perfect spheres" seriously damaged Copernicus's model. In an effort to make the actual observations of planets match his theory, Copernicus had to add back into his scheme some of the epicycles he had been so proud of eliminating, and then move the center of the planets' orbits to a point slightly away from the Sun. Still, he was dissatisfied.

It was this dissatisfaction that kept Copernicus from publishing his theory. By 1531 he had completed *De Revolutionibus Orbium Coelestium* (*On the Revolutions of the Heavenly Spheres*), a book—modeled after Ptolemy's *Almagest*—that proclaimed his heliocentric theory and the mathematics that supported it. But he revealed his ideas to only a few friends. Afraid of publicizing his work until it was free from error, Copernicus continued to make minor corrections and adjustments to his calculations. He may have feared ridicule for inadequately supporting his ideas with observational data, since he had only made 27 observations of his own over the course of 32 years, and most of them were not very good. He based his work mainly on the centuries-old observations of Ptolemy, Hipparchus, Islamic astronomers, and even the ancient Babylonians. Living far from the major academic and publishing centers of his day, and fearing public reaction to such a strange new theory, Copernicus found it easier to keep his work to himself.

Fortunately, Georg Joachim Rheticus, a young mathematician and astronomy professor, heard of Copernicus's theories and in 1539 traveled to meet him. He urged Copernicus to publish and, when Copernicus refused, offered to write a summary of *De Revolutionibus* and publish it under his own name, with a mention of the work of his unnamed mentor. Copernicus reluctantly agreed, Rheticus published his summary (with an apology to Ptolemy), and there was general excitement rather than ridicule.

Copernicus eventually gave in and worked on a final copy of *De Revolutionibus*, which was published in 1543. Copernicus, however, had suffered a stroke, and according to most historical sources he was near death when, on May 24, a copy of his book was finally given to him. The man who reshaped the universe at last held in his hands the work of a lifetime. Within a few hours, he was dead.

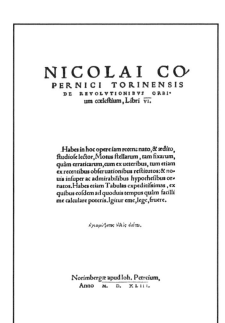

The title page of De Revolutionibus. *Like all scholarly works at the time, it was written in Latin.*

Martin Luther (1483-1546) is famous for his protest against corruption in the Roman Catholic Church, which launched a movement known as the Reformation and led to the founding of the Lutheran Church and other Protestant sects.

The true author of the preface to *De Revolutionibus* was revealed in 1609 by the astronomer Johannes Kepler, who wrote, "It is a most absurd fiction, I admit, that the phenomena of nature can be explained by false causes. But this fiction is not in Copernicus. He thought that these hypotheses were true. . . . Do you wish to know the author of this fiction, which stirs you to such great wrath? Andreas Osiander is named in my copy."

THE RESULT

Ptolemy's vision of Earth at the center of the universe had stood for 1,400 years. It was not until astronomy evolved as a science that such a commonly held belief could fall to truth.

Yet it did not fall without a fight. Although Copernicus's work was initially supported by a number of prominent churchmen and had even been dedicated to Pope Paul III, its new order for the universe was provocative. Hearing of the heliocentric theory in 1533, the Protestant thinker Martin Luther called Copernicus an "upstart astrologer" and commented, "This fool wishes to reverse the entire science of astronomy." Fearing further criticism, Andreas Osiander, a Lutheran clergyman who assisted Rheticus with the publication of *De Revolutionibus*, wrote an anonymous preface to the book stating that heliocentrism was simply a useful tool for making mathematical calculations, not a description of the actual universe. "For these hypotheses," he wrote, "need not be true or even probable." Until more than 60 years later, this preface was mistakenly believed to be written by Copernicus.

Based on the preface, most readers viewed heliocentrism as an unproven theory and concentrated on its practical value. Copernicus's complex mathematical work was highly praised and quickly adopted to create more precise tables for predicting celestial events. It was not until astronomers began to try to prove Copernicus's theory that controversy erupted. In the early seventeenth century, Galileo

Galilei took up the Copernican cause armed with observational evidence. Pope Paul V retaliated by banning *De Revolutionibus*, placing it on a Church list of forbidden books—where it remained until 1835. Copernicus's fear of outrage and ridicule had come true, nearly 80 years after his death. In fact, his heliocentric theory would not be fully accepted as fact for nearly a century after Galileo.

Many elements of Copernicus's model of the solar system, such as circular orbits and epicycles, have been proven incorrect. But although his vision of the universe may not have been perfect, it is certainly familiar. Copernicus was the first to describe the solar system in the general form we know today. In doing so, he opened up our universe. With a heliocentric system, the size of the solar system was not limited by an outer sphere of stars. It was possible that the universe might be much larger than had ever been imagined before.

Like humanity's vision of the universe, astronomy was no longer confined beneath a crystalline ceiling. Having gained the power to challenge strongly held belief with new ideas based on calculation and evidence rather than philosophy and tradition, astronomy had become a true science. And it all started with a quiet man who made only a handful of astronomical observations in his lifetime, but could "see" with the power of mathematics—and who could, eventually, find the courage to tell the world.

ÆTATIS SVÆ ANNOS 0 COMPLE

QVO POST DIVTINVM IN PAT

EXILIVM LIBERTATI DESIDE

DIVINO PROVISV

RESTITVTVS EST

CHAPTER THREE

Tycho Brahe and Observational Astronomy

On the evening of November 11, 1572, the Danish astronomer Tycho Brahe (TY-ko BRAH or BRAH-hee) was walking home from his chemical laboratory to have supper when he happened to glance up at the sky. He couldn't believe what he saw there: a bright light shining in a spot where no star had ever been charted before! Excitedly, he stopped some passers-by and asked them whether they saw the strange light. They did.

Over the next few nights, Tycho watched the skies and was amazed to see that the light did not move. It was not a comet or a meteor, he realized, but a direct challenge to the astronomical theories that had been accepted as fact for centuries. According to the Greek philosopher Aristotle, the terrestrial world of Earth was flawed and impermanent, but the celestial realm of the stars and planets was perfect and unchangeable. Yet here was a great change in the celestial realm—a brand new star in the night sky.

Although his domineering, eccentric, and passionate nature brought Tycho Brahe (1546-1601) little popularity, his obsession with accurate observation of the heavens made him a giant in the field of astronomy.

Clearly something new was brewing on the astronomical horizon, and in response to the flaws that were becoming apparent in the theories of Ptolemy and Aristotle, a different kind of astronomer was called for. For centuries, scientists had reused the same sets of inadequate, inaccurate observations of the heavens. What was needed was a scientist who would use modern tools to thoroughly observe, measure, and record the current motions of the celestial bodies. That position was filled by Tycho Brahe, a man passionate in his quest for precision in his work.

Tyge (later latinized as Tycho) Brahe was one of twins born on December 14, 1546, in Skaane, Denmark (an area now part of Sweden). His father, Otto Brahe, and his mother, Beate Billi, were both from families of Danish nobility. Otto's brother Jörgen had no children, and the two brothers had made an arrangement that if Otto had a son, he would give the child to Jörgen to raise as his own. When Otto's wife delivered twins, the agreement seemed perfect. But one of the twins was stillborn, and Otto refused to give up the other—baby Tycho.

A year later, Otto and Beate had another son. As the story goes, this made the still-childless Jörgen so angry that he kidnapped little Tycho from his natural parents, accusing them of violating their agreement. Although Otto was outraged and ready to retrieve his son, he soon realized that Tycho might benefit from the wealth and opportunities that could be given to him by his powerful uncle Jörgen.

Tycho did benefit from his uncle's care, initially in his education. As a boy, Tycho had a private tutor who taught him to read, write, and speak Latin. At the age of 13, he enrolled in the University of Copenhagen to embark on what his family hoped would be a career in government befitting a nobleman. Much to their disappointment, however, Tycho demonstrated a better aptitude for mathematics than for philosophy, rhetoric, and law. Then, on August 21, 1560, an event occurred that turned Tycho's interest toward a subject outside of the University curriculum—observational astronomy.

Tycho witnessed a partial eclipse of the Sun and was fascinated by the idea that these awesome events could be predicted. With a new-found passion he studied Claudius Ptolemy's great astronomical work, *Almagest*, while ignoring his other studies. Before long, he realized that Ptolemy's predictions were inaccurate and that more reliable records of the positions of the stars were needed.

In 1562, Tycho was sent to the University of Leipzig in Germany to study law. To handle his nephew's money and keep his studies on the right track, Jörgen hired Anders Vedel, a 20-year-old history scholar, as a companion and guardian for Tycho. But even under Vedel's constant supervision, Tycho's interest in astronomy could not be denied. He sought out mathematics and astronomy professors and used his spending money for astronomy books and instruments. During the day, he attended the courses prescribed by his uncle, but at night, while Vedel slept, Tycho secretly studied astronomy.

A conjunction of Saturn and Jupiter in August 1563 further supported Tycho's belief that more

conjunction: the apparent alignment of two or more celestial bodies

accurate observations of the sky were needed. The two accepted tables of planetary movements were shockingly inexact in predicting this event. The thirteenth-century *Alfonsine Tables* (based on Ptolemy's work) were off by an entire month, while the more recent *Prutenic Tables* (based on Copernicus's work) still foretold the conjunction on the wrong day. Tycho decided that new tables needed to be made, based not on a few random observations but on a precise, extensive study of the skies over a long period of time. Only through careful and consistent observation, he believed, could the patterns of the heavens be accurately recorded.

Then in 1565, war broke out between Denmark and Sweden, and Tycho's uncle called him back home. Barely a month after Tycho's return, Jörgen contracted pneumonia and died. Tycho inherited his uncle's great wealth and, after a period of mourning, he returned to Germany free to devote himself to the study of astronomy. He initially enrolled in the University of Wittenberg, but only stayed a few months because of an outbreak of plague. Tycho then transferred farther north to the University of Rostock, where he met another Danish nobleman. The two arrogant, hot-tempered men got into a violent argument over their respective mathematical prowess that nearly led to fistfights on several occasions. Finally, on December 29, 1566, they faced off in a duel with swords. Although neither was killed, Tycho lost a piece of his nose. Fiercely sensitive about his appearance, he had a metal piece made to fit over his disfigured nose.

No drawings or paintings of Tycho show the metal plate he wore over the missing bridge of his nose, since he always insisted that portraits portray him with an intact nose. It was long thought that the metal nose was a composite of gold and silver, but when his tomb was opened in 1901—exactly 300 years after his death—a green stain showed around the upper nasal opening of his skull, indicating the presence of a considerable amount of copper.

Leaving Rostock in 1568, Tycho studied for a brief time at the University of Basel in Switzerland and then lived in Augsburg, Germany. All this time, he made astronomical observations and inscribed the positions of stars and planets as he saw them. It was becoming obvious to Tycho that good observations required good tools, and he began a collection of fine instruments—many of his own design—that would become part of his scientific legacy.

Late in 1570, Otto Brahe fell ill and Tycho was called home to Denmark. When his father died a month later, Tycho shared the inheritance with his brother, Steen, and remained in Denmark to attend to family matters. During this time he became interested in alchemy and chemistry, giving up his astronomical observations until the fateful year of 1572.

Tycho is generally referred to by his first name rather than by his last name.

Among the instruments invented by Tycho was the sextant, which allowed astronomers to measure the angle between two stars. One observer (left) would look along the edge of the instrument and line it up with the spot where a certain star appeared in the sky. The second observer could then sight along an adjustable rod and line it up with a different star. Numbers printed along the rounded edge of the sextant would show, by the position of the rod, the angle between the two stars.

THE BREAKTHROUGH

Amazed, and as if astonished and stupefied, I stood still, gazing for a certain length of time with my eyes fixed intently on it. . . . When I had satisfied myself that no star of that kind had ever shone forth before, I was led to such perplexity by the unbelievability of the thing that I began to doubt the faith of my own eyes.
—Tycho Brahe

When Tycho saw a new star in the constellation Cassiopeia, he knew he had discovered something important. He observed the star until March 1574, when it faded from view. Using one of his instruments, a sextant, he measured the visible distance of the star from the other stars in Cassiopeia and found no change over time, which proved that it was not a moving object. Tycho also recorded its changes in magnitude and color. Over time, the star became dimmer and changed from bright white to yellow to red to dull blue. To modern scientists, these changes identify the phenomenon as a supernova: a distant star, usually invisible to the naked eye, that

Tycho's chart of the position of the suddenly visible star (labeled nova, *the Latin word for "new")*

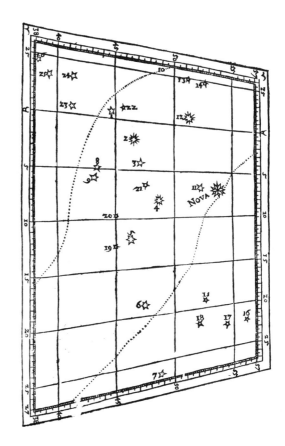

had exploded so forcefully that its light could be seen from Earth. But Tycho only knew he was seeing a new star that did not seem to have existed before, changing in color and brightness, but part of the heavenly realm that Aristotle had taught was unchangeable.

Tycho published a 52-page manuscript on his observations entitled *De Nova Stella* (*The New Star*). Although not altogether a scientific piece (in addition to hard data, it included letters from supportive friends and astrological comments) the book made him famous. In 1575, he traveled to Germany, Switzerland, and Italy to lecture, visit with other astronomers, and inspect their instruments. Tycho was also looking for a place to settle permanently, where his astronomical passion would be welcomed and sponsored by people of power and wealth.

In 1576, King Frederick II of Denmark, a patron of the arts and sciences, made Tycho an extraordinary offer in an effort to keep the astronomer in his native land. The King gave Tycho the island of Hven in the sea north of Copenhagen, along with the funds to establish and maintain an astronomical observatory. The island, approximately 2,000 acres in area, was inhabited by 40 families of farmers living in one village. As lifetime owner of the island, Tycho became their landlord and protector.

Tycho soon began construction of his fabulous observatory, Uraniborg ("Heavenly Castle"), which would become his home for more than 20 years. Although he probably took up residence within months, the building was not finished until 1580

Only three supernovae have been visible from Earth in the last 1,000 years.

Frederick II ruled Denmark from 1559 to 1588.

observatory: a place designed and equipped for making observations of astronomical, meteorological, or other natural phenomena

A drawing of Uraniborg, showing the observatory in the center and the ornamental gardens surrounding it. The complex could be entered by gates at the top and bottom corners; the building at the right corner was the servants' quarters and the one on the left housed a printing press.

and more additions were made thereafter. When completed, Uraniborg was the finest astronomical facility in Europe. It featured fabulously ornate observatories, living accommodations, gardens, a library, a chemical laboratory, a printing press, a private jail, an intercom system, and indoor plumbing. In the library stood a brass globe nearly five feet in diameter, engraved with the zodiac and the exact positions of the fixed stars as Tycho observed them. Elsewhere on the island were a paper mill, a windmill, and workshops where craftsmen made Tycho's astronomical instruments. In 1584, Tycho built a second observatory, Stjerneborg ("Castle of the Stars"), in which the rooms were entirely underground to protect the astronomical instruments from the wind, and the roof could be opened to gain a clear view of the sky.

Tycho's years in Hven were the happiest of his life. He was surrounded by his family—his wife, Christine, whom he had married in 1573, and their eight children—and the brilliant young men who flocked from all over Europe to serve as assistants to the great astronomer. In addition, Tycho hosted a number of important visitors, including the Queen of Denmark, King James I of England, great scientists, and even his old guardian Anders Vedel. In his state-of-the-art observatories, Tycho trained his assistants, designed and tested his instruments, and methodically watched the skies.

This drawing shows two assistants (bottom left and right) and an observer who may be Tycho himself (half-visible on the far right) using an instrument known as a mural quadrant to measure the position of stars. Mounted onto a wall at Uraniborg beneath a large painting of Tycho and various symbols of his work, the quadrant was a quarter-circle made of brass. The observer would look at a star through the window in the left-hand wall and adjust a movable piece of metal to line up with the star. One assistant kept track of the time, while the other recorded the measurements.

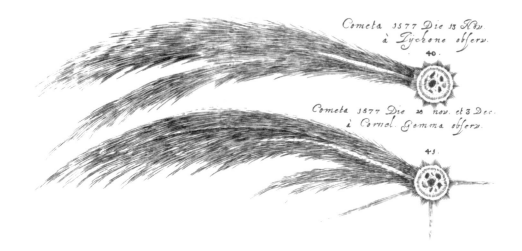

Cometa 1577 Die 13 Nov.
à Tychone obserz.
40.

Cometa 1577 Die 26 nov. et 3 Dec.
à Cornel. Gemma obserz.
45.

Two observations of the comet of 1577

comet: a body made up of dust and ice that moves among the planets. When a comet passes near the Sun, the heat creates a glowing tail of vapor that is often visible from Earth.

Aristotle stated that meteors were also in the terrestrial realm, part of the weather as lightning or tornadoes are. It is due to this belief that the study of the weather is called meteorology.

In only his second year on Hven, on the night of November 13, 1577, Tycho noticed a large comet with a very long tail. He observed the comet until January 1578, when it had become nearly invisible. Because comets moved so erratically—instead of in perfect circular orbits—Aristotle believed that they were located in the terrestrial realm of Earth's atmosphere. But when Tycho measured the comet's apparent size and calculated its distance from Earth, he discovered that it was about three times farther away than the Moon, orbiting the Sun at a distance greater than that of Venus. These observations proved that comets moved among the planets in irregular orbits.

Using his own printing press, Tycho published his complete observational record of the comet in 1588 as the second part of a longer work he planned to call *Astronomiae Instauratae Progymnasmata* (*Introductory Exercises Toward a Restored Astronomy*). Tycho refuted Aristotelian doctrine with his precisely measured proof that the comet moved beyond the Moon. He also included a description of his own system of the universe. Tycho's extensive observations supported the idea that the planets orbited the Sun, but he could not believe Copernicus's theory that Earth also moved. As a compromise, he developed a geoheliocentric model with Earth at rest in the center, orbited by the Sun, Moon, and stars. The other planets then circled the Sun as it moved around the Earth. Although incorrect, Tycho's theory of the universe not only eliminated the epicycles of the Ptolemaic and Copernican models, but also introduced the idea that planets move in orbits that are not solid and might intersect each other, rather than being attached to perfectly centered crystal spheres.

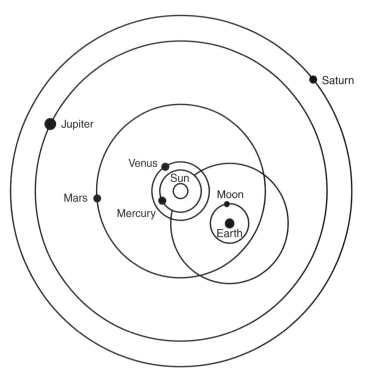

Tycho's model of the universe

THE RESULT

Tycho's system was widely accepted in his day. Mathematically, it functioned correctly, and it provided a handy compromise between the evidence of science and firmly held religious and philosophical beliefs. Yet despite this success, Tycho's career began to decline. With the death in 1588 of his major patron, King Frederick II, he gradually lost favor among the royalty. At first, the new young king, Christian IV, continued to finance the observatory. But Tycho's haughty, often selfish personality and his neglectful treatment of the tenants and public buildings on Hven made him unpopular on the island. This finally came to the attention of King Christian, who cut off Tycho's annual pension. The loss of financial support, perhaps along with his desire to leave the remote island and engage in more intellectual exchange, caused Tycho to retreat into self-imposed exile.

In June 1597, Tycho sailed for Rostock with his family, servants, printing press, and most of his astronomical instruments. He traveled for several years and finished one of his major works, *Astronomiae Instauratae Mechanica* (*Instruments for the Restored Astronomy*), in which he described each of his instruments and their uses. He dedicated this work to the Holy Roman Emperor, Rudolph II, in hopes of impressing him—which he did. In 1599, Rudolph appointed Tycho as Imperial Mathematician at his court in Prague.

Rudolph II (1552-1612) was well educated, but he made a poor ruler because he was often depressed and prone to fits of insanity. By the end of his turbulent reign he had already given up most of his power to his brother and heir, Matthias.

It was in Prague, in a villa belonging to the Emperor, that Tycho set up his instruments for what would be the last time. Late in 1599, he invited a rising astronomer named Johannes Kepler to serve as one of his assistants. Although Tycho resented Kepler's youth and ambition and often treated him rudely, he also recognized that an energetic and talented assistant could be a great help in his work. Kepler and Tycho began to collaborate on a new set of planetary tables based on Tycho's data that would correct the errors of earlier records. The project was called the *Rudolphine Tables*, in honor of the Holy Roman Emperor.

Despite their frequently hostile relationship, it was Kepler to whom Tycho turned in the end. On October 16, 1601, Tycho became suddenly ill at a dinner party and never recovered. On his deathbed, feverish and delirious, he begged Kepler to complete the *Rudolphine Tables*, pleading, "Let me not seem to have lived in vain." On October 23, he died at the age of 54.

Published by Kepler in 1627, the *Rudolphine Tables* were more accurate than any previous planetary tables. But Tycho Brahe's achievement extended far beyond the prediction of conjunctions and eclipses. He thoroughly changed the practice of observation. While other astronomers only watched the planets and the Moon at certain points in their orbits, Tycho kept up constant observations, often discovering orbital abnormalities never before

A monument to Tycho

When Tycho died, Kepler kept his astronomical instruments until Tycho's son-in-law demanded them as part of his inheritance. After being seized from Kepler, they were locked in a vault to rust away for almost 20 years before being destroyed by rioters during a political uprising in Prague. The great brass celestial globe, shown here, was saved and displayed in Copenhagen, but in 1728 it was lost in a fire. Today, not one of Tycho's famous instruments survives. Even Uraniborg was pulled down in 1623 and its stone used in other buildings.

recorded. He also built one of the major research centers of his time and designed astronomical instruments of the highest possible accuracy, bringing the field of astronomy even closer to scientific practice. Most importantly, Tycho never attempted to draw theoretical conclusions on the basis of too few observations or distorted his data to fit his own ideas. In fact, much of his work remained unpublished and uninterpreted during his lifetime. He had gathered the vital data needed to unlock the secrets of the solar system, but someone else would have to open the door and walk through.

CHAPTER FOUR

Johannes Kepler and the Laws of Planetary Motion

When Nicolaus Copernicus, often viewed as the first modern astronomer, suggested that the Sun was at the center of the universe, he never intended to start a revolution. In fact, it was not until 1543, when he was 70 years old, that he finally published his subversive theories about the nature of the heavens. His heliocentric model was an interesting concept that eventually offended just about everyone. And yet, even after Copernicus's death, the revolution that would arise from his theory was still only simmering in the background. After all, intriguing theory or not, few people were willing to go up against the religious and political authorities armed with nothing more than their opinions.

On the other hand, if someone could produce evidence to support a heliocentric theory, then taking on the authorities might not be so dangerous. Fortunately, someone could, and that someone was the Danish astronomer Tycho Brahe. Tycho was

Nervous, moody, sickly, and sarcastic, Johannes Kepler (1571-1630) was an outsider all his life. But even though the world treated him harshly, he remained convinced that the universe was orderly and beautiful— a belief supported by the laws of planetary motion he discovered.

forceful where Copernicus was cautious, boastful where Copernicus was humble. Tycho stormed onto the scene, observing, measuring, and collecting mountains of astronomical data—enough to support a theory, even a revolutionary one. Tycho, however, never published most of his observations, let alone used them to support Copernicus's theory. One more soldier of the scientific revolution was needed to make the connection between Tycho's observations and Copernicus's ideas. That revolutionary was Johannes Kepler, a man who possessed a brilliant mind but was hampered by a hostile personality and trapped in a weak body. He would enter the war reluctantly, and eventually come to know both the triumph and the tragedy of battle.

Johannes Kepler was born almost two months premature on December 27, 1571, in Weil-der-Stadt, Germany. His family included six brothers and sisters, although only three would live to adulthood. His father, Heinrich, born into a once-proud family, had lost his social position and worked as a mercenary soldier. When Johannes was six years old, Heinrich was nearly hanged for a crime he had committed. He escaped punishment, but one day he joined a military campaign in the Netherlands and never returned. Johannes later described his father as "vicious, inflexible, quarrelsome, and doomed to a bad end."

If Johannes's father was hardly the image of the perfect parent, neither was his mother. A superstitious woman who made and sold herbal remedies (a practice that made some people suspect her of witchcraft), Katherine Kepler did not fare much better than Heinrich in her son's memory. "Small, thin, swarthy, gossiping and quarrelsome, of a bad disposition," he described her years later. But, whatever her failings, she did introduce six-year-old Johannes to astronomy by showing him the great comet of 1577.

Often sickly as a child, Johannes endured poor eyesight, boils, rashes, stomach ailments, and a bout of smallpox that nearly killed him. Yet despite it all, he did well in school—at least academically. Socially, growing up was a constant nightmare for Johannes. Friends were hard to come by. Some were probably jealous of his intelligence and performance in school. Others simply found him a weak and easy target. There were also some potential friends, however, who were turned into enemies by Johannes's sarcasm, bragging, and hostility. He had "in every way a dog-like nature," one person remembered about Johannes as a teenager. "He liked gnawing bones and dry crusts of bread and was so greedy that whatever his eyes chanced on he grabbed. . . . He is malicious and bites people with his sarcasms. He hates many people exceedingly, and they avoid him." It is a very unpleasant portrait, especially when you consider that its author is Johannes Kepler himself!

In the sixteenth century, an intelligent but sickly boy was a perfect candidate for the clergy. Accordingly, at 13 years of age, Kepler began his higher education at Germany's Protestant schools. After two years at the seminary in Adelberg and two more at Maulbronn, he moved on to the German University of Tübingen.

astrology: the study of the positions of the Sun, Moon, stars, and planets in the belief that they influence earthly events and human fortunes

A horoscope chart drawn by Kepler

At Tübingen, Kepler was influenced by the astronomy professor Michael Maestlin. Although knowledge of heliocentric theory was frowned upon by the Lutheran leaders of the university, Maestlin was familiar with Copernicus's ideas, having carefully read and annotated his book *De Revolutionibus*. While forced to teach the geocentrism of Ptolemy to his students, Maestlin privately convinced Kepler that Copernicus's model of the universe must be true.

In 1594, with only six months left before becoming a man of the church, Kepler was sent off to teach at the Lutheran school in the Austrian town of Graz. The local mathematics teacher there had died, and officials from the University of Tübingen recommended Kepler to replace him. He did not want to go, but he had little choice in the matter. The university officials knew of Kepler's interest in mathematics, and they suspected he had little future as a minister. They wanted him off their hands.

Kepler did not amount to much as a teacher and had few students. The 22-year-old filled his empty hours by designing horoscopes and almanacs. Kepler was more interested in astronomy than astrology, but he had a mystical streak, and besides, it was astrology that paid the bills. As he once remarked, "God provides for every animal his means of sustenance. For the astronomer, He has provided astrology." This statement proved especially true for Kepler in 1595, when one of his astrological calendars predicted a cold winter and an invasion by the Turks. By a stroke of sheer luck for Kepler, both of these events came to pass. His reputation began to grow, and he looked for a way to merge his two interests, astrology and astronomy, into a theory of the universe.

Kepler's work in mathematics reinforced his long-held belief that the universe should be perfect. He sought in the heavens the same symmetry and harmony he saw in the study of geometry. He thought there must, for example, be a mathematical reason why there were exactly six planets. (There are more than six planets, of course, but no one knew that at the time.) And, Kepler believed, there must be a reason that each planet was located at a certain distance from the Sun.

There were only five perfect polyhedrons, or three-dimensional shapes, in geometry, and it seemed to Kepler that such things did not happen by chance. Perhaps, he thought, these shapes might represent the geometric relationships between the planets' orbits. He found that if he drew the sphere that represented the orbital path of Mercury, then encased it in an octahedron, and then drew a second sphere around the outside of the octahedron, that second sphere would contain the orbital path of Venus. If he encased that sphere in an icosahedron, the next sphere would be the orbit of Earth—and so on out to the orbit of Saturn, using a different polyhedron to separate each planet from the next.

Everything seemed to fit. Kepler believed he had found the mathematical harmony of the universe. "I no longer regretted the time wasted," he wrote in his journal. "Within a few days everything

By the way, so far the calendar's predictions are proving correct. There is an unheard-of cold in our land. In the Alpine farms, people die of the cold. It is reliably reported that when they arrive home and blow their noses, the noses fall off. . . . As for the Turks, they devastated the whole country.
—Johannes Kepler, in a letter to Michael Maestlin

polyhedron: a solid figure, such as a cube, that is made up of polygons (flat shapes made of straight lines, like a square). The five perfect polyhedrons, also called Platonic solids, are: tetrahedron, cube, octahedron, dodecahedron, and icosahedron.

physics: the science that studies the interactions of matter and energy, and attempts to describe them in terms of simple laws

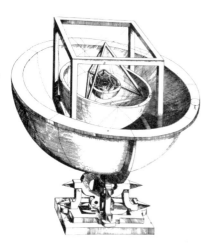

Kepler's diagram of his theory from Mysterium Cosmographicum. *The outermost sphere is the orbit of Saturn, and inscribed inside it (placed so that its corners touch the sphere) is a cube. Inscribed within that cube is a sphere that represents the orbit of Jupiter; inscribed within that sphere is a tetrahedron, and so forth.*

worked, and I watched as one body after another fit precisely into its place among the planets."

Kepler's theory was dead wrong, but it did have one redeeming quality: it only worked with the Sun at the center. In fact, while he was forming his model of the universe Kepler had begun to think about the movement of the planets in terms of physics. He thought that perhaps the Sun generated a magnetic force that attracted and repelled the planets, causing them to move in their orbits.

Kepler published his geometric theory in 1596 as *Mysterium Cosmographicum* (*Cosmographic Mystery*), and his ingenious mathematics gained him credibility in the scientific community. He sent copies to famous astronomers of the day, including Galileo Galilei and Tycho Brahe. Tycho even invited Kepler to visit him at his great observatory on the island of Hven, but Kepler decided the journey was too far.

The next year, Kepler married Barbara Müller. Their marriage soon frustrated him, however, when he realized that his wife understood very little of his life's work (he once spitefully described her as "simple of mind and fat of body"). Frustration became grief with the early death of their first two children. Yet these personal difficulties, along with financial troubles and growing religious persecution, did have the effect of pushing Kepler to make a change. In 1599, after the Catholic leaders of Graz closed the Protestant school and banished its ministers and teachers, Kepler traveled to Prague in the hope of increasing his income by joining with Tycho Brahe, who was now the royal astronomer of Holy Roman Emperor Rudolph II.

Kepler longed for complete access to Tycho's vast collection of data, especially when he realized that Tycho had failed to make much use of his own observations. "Tycho possesses the best observations," Kepler noted. "He only lacks the architect who would put all this to use according to his own design." Kepler longed to be that architect, using Tycho's work to support his own theory of the universe. But although Tycho welcomed Kepler as an assistant, he revealed very little of his scientific journals. He respected Kepler's mind, but he tried his best not to show it. To keep his brash young assistant busy, he assigned him a puzzle that no other astronomer, including Tycho, had been able to solve: calculating the orbit of Mars. Kepler bragged that he could finish the job in eight days, but in reality it would take him closer to six years.

The year 1600 was wrought with quarrels and then reconciliations between the two scientific geniuses. Kepler was also occupied with personal and financial worries that had him traveling between Graz and Prague. Then suddenly, in 1601, Kepler's status took a turn. Tycho Brahe died, and within days Kepler was appointed to take over as Imperial Mathematician of the Holy Roman Empire. Kepler also took over Tycho's instruments and the one thing he coveted: Tycho's observational manuscripts. He finally had what he needed to prove how the planets orbited the Sun.

Tycho gave me no opportunities to share in his experiences. He would only in the course of a meal, and in between conversing about other matters, mention, as if in passing, today the figure for the apogee [the point of an orbit furthest from the Sun] of the planet, tomorrow the nodes [the points where an orbit crosses Earth's orbit] of another.

—Johannes Kepler

THE BREAKTHROUGH

In the beginning, progress was slow. Kepler was plagued by ill health and constantly distracted from his work by official duties, such as writing annual astrological calendars, casting horoscopes for visiting dignitaries, and making comments on important heavenly events. He was building a reputation, but not much of an income. Rudolph II's authority was waning, and he could not be counted on for a regular salary. Then Tycho's heirs began demanding their inheritance, and Kepler was forced to give up all of Tycho's valuable instruments. Furthermore, determining the orbit of Mars was becoming a nightmare. Kepler tested 70 different circular orbits against Tycho's data, but no matter how he adjusted them, his results did not match the observations. Forced to try something new, Kepler imagined himself viewing Earth's orbit from Mars. But although his calculations covered more than 900 pages, they revealed no answer.

It was frustrating work, and eventually Kepler was forced to turn away from the one assumption that had been holding him back. Desperate for a new approach, he tried to imagine the movement of Mars as seen from the Sun. Suddenly, his calculations made sense. "I have the answer!" he wrote. "The orbit of the planet is a perfect ellipse."

To show how Copernicus's heliocentric solar system operated, Kepler needed to leap beyond accepted truth. "My first mistake was in having assumed that the orbit on which planets move is a

Ah, what a foolish bird I had been.
—Johannes Kepler, on realizing that planetary orbits are elliptical

circle," Kepler admitted. "This mistake . . . had been supported by the authority of all the philosophers." When Kepler imagined orbits of a different shape, he could begin the work that would change the way everyone thought about the universe—forever. Modern scientists have labeled the resulting breakthroughs "Kepler's Laws of Planetary Motion." Kepler published the work behind the first two laws, along with other findings, in his 1609 book *Astronomia Nova* (*The New Astronomy*).

Kepler's first law states that the orbit of a planet is an ellipse. The problem of predicting a planet's orbit mathematically had been created by the assumption that orbits were circular, with the Sun at the center of the circle. An ellipse is an oval-shaped orbit with two centers (called *foci*, the plural of focus).

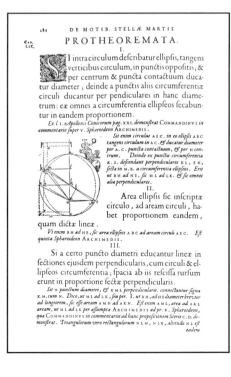

The page of Astronomia Nova *in which Kepler explained (in Latin) his first two laws of planetary motion. The diagram shows the orbit of Mars around the Sun.*

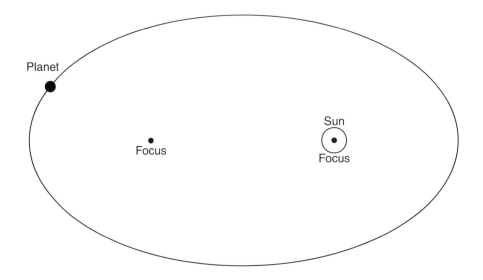

A diagram of Kepler's first law, with the shape of the ellipse exaggerated to make it more visible. It took astronomers so long to figure out the shape of planetary orbits because most of them are only slightly elliptical. If Tycho had assigned him to study the motion of Venus, Kepler might never have made his discovery. Mars, however, has a much more pronounced elliptical orbit than other planets do.

The Sun is at one focus of a planet's elliptical orbit, and the other focus is an imaginary point in space.

Once Kepler saw the orbits as ellipses, other observations and calculations began to make sense. For example, at the point in Mars's orbit when it is closest to the Sun, its speed is faster than when it is farther from the Sun. Understanding that the orbit was an ellipse allowed Kepler to see the connection between orbital speed and closeness to the Sun, which led directly to his second law. This states that the orbital speed of a planet is greatest when the planet is closest to the Sun. But although the speed varies throughout an orbit, Kepler found that the motion of planets follows a simple mathematical rule: a planet will move through equal areas in its orbital plane over equal periods of time.

As a matter of fact, orbital speed can be determined for a planet if its distance from the Sun is

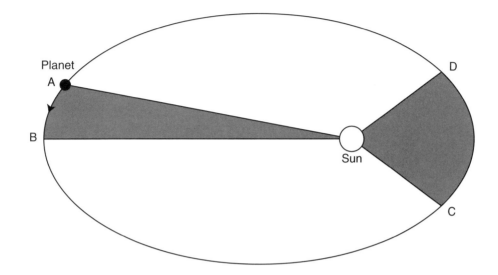

known, and distance from the Sun can be calculated if the planet's orbital speed is known. Kepler developed this formula and published it a decade later in his *Harmonice Mundi* (*The Harmony of the World*). It is still useful for calculating orbital speeds of planets, moons, asteroids, comets, and even artificial satellites. Called Kepler's third law, the mathematical formula states that the cube of the distance of a body from the Sun is proportional (related) to the square of its orbital period (the amount of time it takes to orbit the Sun once). In other words, the distance of each planet from the Sun determines how long that planet takes to revolve around the Sun.

Kepler now knew that the Sun regulated the velocity and motion of the planets. The universe was beginning to make sense.

A diagram of Kepler's second law. Kepler found that if a planet takes the same amount of time to travel the distance from A to B as it does from C to D, the area of the two shaded spaces will be equal.

THE RESULT

As the young science of astronomy expanded, Kepler remained in the forefront. He studied optics; after Galileo used a telescope to discover four objects orbiting Jupiter in 1610, Kepler invented a telescope using two convex lenses and developed a formula for determining a lens' power of magnification.

Gathering together the data of two lifetimes—his own and Tycho's—Kepler published an extensive collection of new tables of planetary motion. The *Rudolphine Tables* appeared in 1627, named in honor of the emperor who had died 15 years earlier. For many people, predicting celestial events more accurately was the true test of Kepler's laws of planetary motion, and his theories endured the challenge. Far more precise than any previously published, his

Although Rudolph II was a learned man, it is unlikely that—as this illustration suggests—he and Kepler regularly discussed astronomy together. By the time Kepler began work on the Rudolphine Tables, *the emperor had become mentally unstable and was losing his ruling power to his brother Matthias.*

tables were basic to the research of astronomers throughout the Renaissance and into the modern age.

And yet in the life of Johannes Kepler, triumph always seemed to be mixed with tragedy. A smallpox epidemic claimed the life of his favorite son in 1611, and soon afterward Kepler's wife died of typhus. Rudolph abdicated the throne that same year and died a year later, ending Kepler's hope for financial comfort. In 1615, Kepler received news that his mother was being charged with witchcraft. Over the next six years, she was repeatedly interrogated, imprisoned, tried in court, and threatened with torture. Kepler defended her tirelessly, spending months studying the case and often traveling to Württemberg to appear in court. The charges were eventually dropped, but Katherine Kepler died six months after her release.

Even though he found comfort with a second wife and family and received professional recognition with the publication of several additional books, Kepler remained desperate for financial security for himself and his family. He would never really be happy. Traveling to Linz in 1630 to try to collect salary that was owed him, Johannes Kepler became acutely ill with a fever and died on November 18. In his last moments, the tragic and triumphant revolutionary silently pointed his finger first to his head, then to the sky. The epitaph for his tombstone was in his own words:

> I measured the skies, now I measure the shadows
> Skybound was the mind, the body rests in the earth.

In 1631, for the first time in recorded history, Mercury was observed crossing the face of the Sun—as predicted in the *Rudolphine Tables*. Kepler's calculations of the event were found to be 30 times more accurate than those in previous tables.

A local judge expressed his opinion that the worst part of Katherine Kepler's case was the arrogant son who defended her. The court record from the hearings reads, "The accused appeared in court, accompanied, alas, by her son, Johannes Kepler, mathematician."

Kepler's grave was trampled and destroyed in the Thirty Years' War.

CHAPTER FIVE

Galileo Galilei
and the Telescope

In 1609, when Johannes Kepler published his first two laws of planetary motion, the science of astronomy was still an uncomfortable combination of abstract mathematics, primitive observation, and religious belief. Nowhere was the conflict more strongly evident than in Italy, the seat of the Roman Catholic Church. The Church still instructed its followers in a geocentric (Earth-centered) universe based on the ancient ideas of Aristotle and Claudius Ptolemy. The heliocentric (Sun-centered) theory proposed in 1543 by Nicolaus Copernicus was considered just that—a theory. No one had been able to produce concrete evidence that proved the solar system was heliocentric because until this time, observation of the skies was limited to what could be seen by the naked eye. But another world beyond these physical limitations was about to open up—and it would happen right before the eyes of the religious authorities.

By improving astronomy's power to observe the heavens, Galileo Galilei (1564-1642) transformed the theories of Copernicus into a religious and scholarly controversy that would rage for years.

75

Galileo Galilei was born in Pisa, Italy, on February 15, 1564. He was the oldest of seven children born to Guilia Ammananti and Vincenzo Galilei, a poor but accomplished musician who traded in wool to make ends meet. Vincenzo belonged to a circle of experimental musicians and occasionally performed in the court of the Grand Duke of Tuscany. From his father, Galileo inherited a confrontational temper, a sarcastic sense of humor, and a profound skepticism toward traditional ways of thought. Once, in a controversy with another scholar over musical theory, Vincenzo devised experiments to show the relation between sound, length, and tension of the strings of musical instruments, and it is likely that this early exposure to physical observation was not lost on Galileo. A firm belief in experimentation shaped Galileo's future as a respected teacher and scientist, but it would later involve him in conflict and professional humiliation.

From 1575 to 1579, Galileo was educated by the Vallombrosan monks at a school near Florence, where Vincenzo had moved with his family. But when Galileo announced his intention to become a monk himself, his father withdrew him from the school. At 17, with his father's encouragement, Galileo enrolled in the University of Pisa as a medical student. His commitment to medicine was not great, however. More interested in mathematics, he secretly received private instruction from Ostilio Ricci, the official mathematician of the Tuscan court. When his father's money ran out in 1585, Galileo left the university without a degree and returned to

It appears to me that they who rely simply on the weight of authority to prove any assertion, without searching out the arguments to support it, act absurdly. I wish to question freely and to answer freely.
—Vincenzo Galilei

Despite his indifference to the study of medicine, as a student at Pisa Galileo invented the pulsiogium—a pendulum that doctors could use to measure the pulse of a patient.

Florence to tutor students and continue his studies of the Greek mathematicians Euclid and Archimedes. During this time, Galileo's interest in the physics of the natural world and the testing of mathematical rules began to take hold. He sought a position at a university, and in 1589 was awarded the post of professor of mathematics at the University of Pisa.

Galileo was popular with his students in Pisa, but with other professors his relationships were not so cordial. He campaigned to discredit Aristotelian physics in a mocking and argumentative manner. From this time a dramatic story evolved concerning Galileo, the Leaning Tower of Pisa, and a particular Aristotelian theory. Although the anecdote is not given much credit today, it does contain a grain of truth about the passion with which Galileo attacked the old laws of physics. Aristotle theorized that two objects dropped from the same height would hit the ground at different times, depending on their respective weights. An early biographer wrote that the brash Galileo dropped two cannonballs of different weights from the top of the Leaning Tower of Pisa, noting that, contrary to Aristotle's belief, they both hit the ground at the same time. Galileo's alleged demonstration proved the theory that bodies of the same material but of different weights fall with equal speed.

In reality, Galileo experimented with this physical law by rolling balls of different weights down an inclined plane. Since in his day the measurement of small units of time was limited to the beat of a pulse or the dripping of water, the rate of motion of a

physics: the science that studies the interactions of matter and energy, and attempts to describe them in terms of simple laws

Although Galileo never married, during his time in Padua he had two daughters and a son with a woman named Marina Gamba. When Marina married another man, Galileo sent his daughters to a convent, where they suffered great poverty and hardship. Virginia (the eldest daughter) established a strong relationship with her father in his old age, but her sister, Livia, never forgave Galileo's years of neglect.

body in free fall was much too fast to be timed accurately. Galileo made the slope of his ramp gentle enough to slow the motion of a rolling body to a rate he could measure. The outcome was the same—how fast an object fell was independent of its weight.

Vincenzo Galilei died in 1591, leaving his eldest son with the burden of financially supporting his sisters, as well as his irresponsible brother, Michelangelo. Galileo's salary at the university was not substantial and he had alienated many faculty members. It was time to move on. In 1592, he accepted a position at the University of Padua in the Free Republic of Venice, where he lived and taught for the next 18 years. It was a productive period in Galileo's life, since the liberal, intellectual atmosphere of Padua attracted the best scholars from all over Italy.

Galileo lectured on Euclid and Ptolemy and gave private instruction in military engineering, mechanics, and possibly astronomy—although there is no evidence that he was deeply interested in the subject at this time. During these years, he also thought up an explanation for the movement of the tides, experimented with the pendulum, developed a machine to irrigate crops, invented a primitive thermometer, and improved the sector, a mathematical instrument used to measure angles. Always interested in turning his inventions to practical use and financial gain, Galileo marketed his devices to royal patrons, engineers, and military officials.

In 1597, the young astronomer Johannes Kepler sent Galileo a copy of his book *Mysterium*

Cosmographicum, which was based on the idea of a heliocentric universe. Although Galileo apparently did not bother to read the book, he did correspond briefly with Kepler about the theories of Copernicus, claiming that he supported them but feared to speak out. Kepler replied, "Have faith, Galileo, and come forward!"

It was not until 1604, however, that Galileo began to make public declarations of his rebellious opinions about astronomy. In that year, the appearance of a "new star" (actually a supernova) seen by astronomers all over Europe led to disputes about Aristotle's theory that the heavens were perfect, eternal, and unchangeable. In a series of three lectures at the university, Galileo positioned himself strongly against the concept of an unchangeable universe. Soon, however, the debates over the meaning of celestial appearances would involve more than what could be seen with the naked eye. In 1608, a Dutch spectacle-maker named Hans Lippershey invented the spyglass, an instrument that consisted of a wooden tube fitted with two lenses (curved pieces of glass) to make distant objects appear closer. It was this device that led Galileo Galilei to his destiny in the history of astronomy.

I have not dared to publish, fearful of meeting the same fate as our master Copernicus, who, although he has earned himself immortal fame amongst a few, yet among the greater number appears as only worthy of hooting and derision; so great is the number of fools. I should indeed dare to bring forward my speculations if there were many like you; but since there are not, I shrink from a subject of this description.
—Galileo, in a letter to Johannes Kepler

THE BREAKTHROUGH

When Galileo heard of Lippershey's invention, he hastened to construct his own instrument before anyone could beat him to it. Determined to profit from the new technology, he demonstrated his spyglass to Venetian officials. They were impressed by its military and commercial usefulness, for they could now spot a ship in the distance two hours before it could be seen by the naked eye. Galileo was rewarded with a lifetime tenure at the University of Padua and a doubled salary. By the end of 1609, he had improved upon the spyglass to the point that it could magnify the image of an object 20 times. Then one night he turned his instrument to the skies, and the age of telescopic astronomy began.

Galileo's telescopes were refracting telescopes, in which two pieces of curved glass (lenses)—one at each end of a long tube—gather and focus light to magnify distant objects.

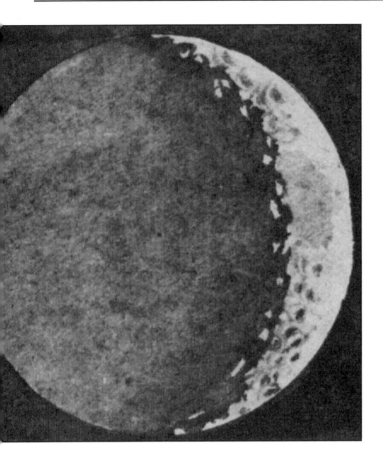

One of Galileo's drawings of the mountains on the Moon

Immediately, Galileo saw that the sky was not a single layer or sphere of stars. Ranging deep out into space, the stars were far more numerous than anyone had suspected; in a single night, he observed 80 new stars in the constellation Orion. Galileo also found that the Moon was mountainous, the Sun had spots, and the Milky Way was not a cloud but a myriad of separate stars. His discoveries challenged Aristotle's view that Earth was the only part of the universe without a smooth, unblemished surface.

I have observed the nature and material of the Milky Way. . . . The galaxy is, in fact, nothing but a congeries [collection] of innumerable stars grouped together in clusters. Upon whatever part of it the telescope is directed, a vast crowd of stars is immediately presented to view.
—Galileo Galilei

Galileo (center, standing with raised arm) demonstrates his telescope to an amazed audience.

Galileo also noted the oval appearance of Saturn. His telescope was not powerful enough, however, to discern that the oval shape was due to Saturn's rings. The rings of Saturn were not discovered until 1655, when they were observed by Christiaan Huygens.

On January 7, 1610, Galileo observed Jupiter in the midst of three stars that were visible only through the telescope and were arranged in a perfectly straight line. Over the next several nights, he saw that these stars sometimes appeared to the west of Jupiter and sometimes to the east; one night there were only two stars, and by January 13 there were four. Eventually, Galileo realized that the objects were not stars, but small bodies orbiting Jupiter just as the Moon orbits Earth. With excitement and haste, Galileo published a 24-page account of his observations, entitled *Sidereus Nuncius* (*The Starry Messenger*). In it, he concluded that Jupiter and its orbiting moons were a miniature model of a Copernican solar system, and proof that the entire universe did not revolve around Earth.

Published in March 1610, the book made Galileo famous. All 500 copies sold out almost instantly. Johannes Kepler, who by this time was recognized as a great astronomer, endorsed Galileo enthusiastically. After naming the moons of Jupiter after the Grand Duke of Tuscany, Cosimo de Medici, Galileo was appointed Philosopher and Mathematician to the Tuscan court in Florence. In 1611, he was honored in Rome for his work with the telescope. At a banquet, guests used a telescope to read an inscription on a building a mile away and then viewed Jupiter and its moons. Even the Catholic Church celebrated Galileo's accomplishments. After a group of Jesuit mathematicians tested Galileo's observations and found them to be accurate, the scholarly Cardinal Robert Bellarmine held

O telescope, instrument of much knowledge, more precious than any scepter! . . . How the subtle mind of Galileo, in my opinion the first philosopher of the day, uses this telescope of ours like a sort of ladder, scales the furthest and loftiest walls of the visible world, surveys all things with his own eyes.
—Johannes Kepler, in a
   letter to Galileo

Galileo called the moons of Jupiter the "Medicean planets," but Johannes Kepler thought there should be a distinction between planets, which orbit the Sun, and moons, which orbit other planets. He suggested the word "satellite" (from the Greek satellos, *which means "attendant") to describe the moons. Today, "satellite" is used to refer to any smaller body that orbits a larger one, and Jupiter's moons—shown here as they appeared to Jesuit observers in 1620—are known as the Galilean satellites.*

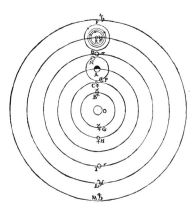

Galileo's model of the universe was similar to Copernicus's, but it made the important innovation of showing that Earth is not the only planet orbited by a satellite.

a reception in his honor. Galileo also met Cardinal Maffeo Barberini, an important and intelligent man with whom he formed a respectful friendship.

But while almost everyone accepted Galileo's observations, many attacked his Copernican interpretation of his discoveries. Studying the planet Venus closely, Galileo had found that it had Moon-like phases (sometimes appearing in the sky as a thin crescent and sometimes as a full circular disk) and that it appeared closer in its crescent phase than when it was full. If the solar system were geocentric, Venus would always be between Earth and the Sun, so that its illuminated side would face away from Earth and it would never appear full. Thus, Galileo concluded (correctly) that Venus and Earth are both orbiting the Sun; sometimes Venus is between Earth and the Sun (appearing as a crescent close to Earth) and sometimes it is on the opposite side of the Sun than Earth is (appearing full and farther away).

Galileo stated his beliefs plainly in *Sidereus Nuncius*: "With absolute necessity we shall conclude, in agreement with the theories of . . . Copernicus, that Venus revolves around the Sun just as do all the other planets." His early reluctance to speak out publicly in support of Copernican theory had been overcome once he was convinced by the observational evidence. Although his friends advised him to proceed cautiously, Galileo forged ahead in his quest to have Copernican theory accepted as fact by religious and academic authorities. Unfortunately, this aggressive crusade would bring him years of persecution from the strong arm of an angry Church.

THE RESULT

Because heliocentrism did not seem to match the information about the universe that was written in the Bible, the Roman Catholic Church continued to reject Copernican theory. Galileo was a pious man who wanted to obey the Church; before publishing his *Letters on Sunspots* in 1613, he cautiously wrote to a Church leader to find out what the Bible had to say about the perfection of the heavens and the motion of the Earth. But Galileo's belief in his observations was too strong, and so was his temper. He could not resist attacking and ridiculing those who believed blindly in the Aristotelian system, and this earned him many enemies within the Church.

By 1615, Galileo found himself traveling to Rome to defend himself against accusations of heresy (statements against Church doctrine). His effort, however, reaped the opposite effect. In arguing his case, Galileo pointed out ways that Scripture could be reinterpreted to support Copernican theory. This was strictly against the laws of the Church, which dictated that only members of the clergy could interpret the Bible. Irritated by Galileo's arrogance, in 1616 Pope Paul V banned Copernicus's book *De Revolutionibus*. He then declared that Galileo was forbidden to hold, teach, or defend Copernican ideas.

On the pope's orders, Cardinal Bellarmine invited Galileo to his home and told him to stop publicly defending Copernican theory. Since Galileo never received a written message from the pope, it is likely that he misinterpreted his conversation with

St. Robert Bellarmine (1542-1621) joined the Jesuit order of the Church in 1560 and became a cardinal in 1599. A great religious scholar, Bellarmine was a central figure in the Catholic Reformation, the Church's response to the growing Protestant movement of the sixteenth century. He was canonized (declared a saint) in 1930.

Some, through their imprudent behavior, have brought things to such a point that the reading of the work of Copernicus, which remained absolutely free for eighty years, is now prohibited.
—Johannes Kepler

Bellarmine as a private warning, not a formal papal decree. Unfortunately, he deluded himself into believing that he had escaped punishment and was not in further danger.

Galileo spent the next seven years trying to follow Bellarmine's advice. He took up noncontroversial problems, such as determining longitudes at sea. Then, in 1623, Galileo believed there was hope for change in policy when his old friend Cardinal Barberini was elected to be the next pope, Urban VIII. Galileo returned to Rome in 1624 to pay his respects to the new pope and was warmly received. He was even granted permission to express the ideas of the Copernican system in a book, on the condition that he gave equal discussion to the theories of Aristotle and left the final conclusion up to the reader.

Pope Urban VIII (1568-1644)

For the next six years, Galileo was occupied with this literary work, which he called *The Dialogue Concerning the Two Chief World Systems*. The book took the form of a fictional discussion between a spokesman for Copernicus, a spokesman for Aristotle, and a third person from whom the other two were hoping to gain support for their views. The conversation between the men lasted four days and covered the "two chief world systems" from all directions. Rather than writing in scholarly Latin, Galileo chose to use Italian to appeal to a wider audience.

Throughout the *Dialogue*, Galileo's bias against the theories of Aristotle was obvious. Simplicio, the man who represented the Aristotelians, was presented as a fool who asked silly questions and made senseless arguments, while Salviati, the Copernican

character, was a witty genius. Salviati rejected
Aristotle's idea of an unchanging universe by point-
ing out the "new stars" of 1572 and 1604 and the
mountains on the Moon, and he explained the daily
motions of the heavens by declaring that Earth
rotates on its axis. To this, the foolish Simplicio
replied that if the world were turning, then anything
not fastened down (like clouds and birds) would be
left behind as Earth rotated. By the end of the dialogue, Salviati and the "neutral" participant, Sagredo,
were ganging up on Simplicio, who himself seemed
to begin to doubt Aristotelian beliefs.

Pope Urban VIII was furious when the
Dialogue was published in 1632. Many of the official
Roman Catholic ideas about the universe, including
some arguments that Urban himself had used in private conversations with Galileo, had been put in the

The title page of Galileo's
Dialogue Concerning the
Two Chief World Systems

The Inquisition was most active in southern France, northern Italy, and Germany during the Middle Ages. Although much less harsh than the infamous Spanish Inquisition (which was an entirely separate institution), the Inquisition was known to torture people who were accused of heresy. This drawing shows fifteenth-century heretics being nailed to wooden posts.

mouth of the ridiculous Simplicio. Insulted and betrayed, the pope was ready to listen to enemies of Galileo who wanted to charge the astronomer with heresy. When Urban discovered—probably from a forged document—that his predecessor, Paul V, had forbidden Galileo to support Copernican theory in 1616, he had the excuse he needed to take action.

Galileo was ordered to stand trial before the Inquisition, a Church tribunal that had been established in the thirteenth century for the discovery and punishment of heretics. The Church argued that Galileo had broken his vow of silence on discussing Copernican theory. Galileo believed that he was innocent because he had not spoken out in direct defense of Copernicus. Aging, ill, and threatened with torture, however, he was persuaded that he

had gone too far in his arguments. In a formal ceremony on June 22, 1633, at the Dominican convent of Santa Maria Sopra Minerva in Rome, Galileo got down on his knees and renounced his beliefs.

Like Copernicus's book *De Revolutionibus*, Galileo's *Dialogue* was put on the Church's Index of Prohibited Books, and Galileo was sentenced to permanent house arrest. He spent the remaining eight years of his life in a villa outside Florence, with his daughter Virginia as his companion. In 1638, he completed a new book, *Discourses on Two New Sciences*, which contained many of his theories of physics; the book was smuggled out of the country and published in the Protestant Netherlands, beyond the reach of the Catholic Church. Galileo continued to observe the Moon and planets through his telescope until he lost his sight. Five years later, in January 1642, he died at the age of 77.

It was an undeserved end for a man who had pushed the vision of scientists and explorers deeper into space. Never again would astronomers depend purely on naked-eye examination of the stars; the rules and the tools of astronomy had changed. But even though he did much to broaden the acceptance of Copernican theory, the full force of Galileo's influence on the scientific world would not be felt until much later. His quest to prove the truth of a heliocentric universe would be passed on, to be taken up almost immediately in the distant northern country of England—beyond the strict control of the Catholic Church—by a mathematical genius named Isaac Newton.

Of his blindness, Galileo lamented, "This universe that I have extended a thousand times . . . has now shrunk to the narrow confines of my own body."

In 1979, Pope John Paul II ordered a Church commission to study the records of Galileo's trial. On October 31, 1992, he issued a formal announcement acknowledging Galileo's suffering at the hands of the Church and admitting misjudgments may have been made in the case.

CHAPTER SIX

Isaac Newton
and Universal Gravitation

On January 8, 1642, the great astronomer Galileo Galilei died in Florence, Italy. The seasons passed to summer and once again to winter. Then, in Woolsthorpe, England, on Christmas Day in the very year of Galileo's death, a child was born prematurely and was not expected to live. His name was Isaac Newton.

Even in the mid-seventeenth century, astronomy had not yet been fully accepted as a science. Galileo had developed a new astronomical tool, the telescope, and made significant discoveries with it, but he had also paid a price for his innovations. Although he was certain that he had found evidence to support Copernicus's heliocentric theory, the powerful Roman Catholic Church had forced him to deny his belief that Earth—like all the other planets—orbited the Sun. People continued to study his work, as well as that of Copernicus and Kepler, but the fact remained that none of these astronomers

"I do not know what I may appear to the world," said Isaac Newton (1642-1727), who singlehandedly developed mathematical laws to prove the theories of Copernicus, Kepler, and Galileo, "but to myself I seem to have been only a boy playing on the seashore, and diverting myself in now and then finding a smoother pebble or a prettier shell than ordinary, whilst the great ocean of truth lay all undiscovered before me."

had been able to fully support their theories at the level of mathematical proof. And without proof, a theory remains only a theory.

Isaac Newton would eventually be the one to provide that proof. But at first, life presented more immediate challenges. Isaac Newton senior, an illiterate farmer, had died two months before his son's birth. The newborn Isaac was so small that his mother, Hannah, claimed he could have fit into a quart bottle. Then, when Isaac was only three years old, Hannah married the Reverend Barnabas Smith and left her son in the care of his grandparents. Isaac was raised within sight of the home of his mother, his stepfather, and their three children, but had little or no contact with them.

The separation came to an end in 1653, when Reverend Smith died and Hannah reunited with Isaac, who was now 11 years old. But never knowing his father and feeling rejected by his mother had a profound effect on Isaac's personality. He resented his mother's actions and was jealous of his stepfather, even years after Smith's death. As a young man of 19, Isaac made a list of his secret sins, one of which was "Threatening my father and mother Smith to burne them and the house over them."

Even at a young age, Isaac showed interest and talent in developing mechanical devices. He designed models, clocks, windmills, sundials, and kites lifted by flaming lanterns that more than once terrified the neighbors. Soon after his mother returned to him, Isaac was sent to King's School in the nearby town of Grantham. Although his teachers quickly recognized

Among young Isaac's other "sins" were "peevishness with my mother," "punching my sister," and "wishing death and hoping it to some."

his potential, Hannah saw little value in higher education and withdrew him from school after four years to make a farmer of him. Isaac, however, was completely uninterested in farming. After one too many incidents in which he was caught reading or daydreaming while he was supposed to be tending the livestock, Hannah gave in and sent him off to Trinity College at Cambridge University.

Arriving in Cambridge in 1661, Isaac Newton immersed himself in the academic world and developed into a serious student. He studied everything from language to alchemy to perpetual motion devices—all with the same intensity. As his studies progressed, he also became more withdrawn and eccentric. He would often skip meals, apparently forgetting about them. Once, while working on a difficult problem, he found that he could not concentrate and complained that he was losing his mental ability. When he suddenly realized that he had not slept for days, he reluctantly gave in and went to bed.

After earning his Bachelor of Arts degree from Trinity College in 1665, Newton was preparing to continue his education in Cambridge when the university was suddenly shut down due to an outbreak of the plague. Isaac returned to his mother's home in the countryside of Lincolnshire and stayed there for the next two years. "In those days," he later said, "I was in the prime of my age for invention and minded Mathematicks and Philosophy more than at any time since." He was the right person in the right place at the right time. Then the last piece fell into place.

It was an apple.

alchemy: an early form of chemistry with philosophical and magical associations; alchemists sought to change base metals into gold and give human beings immortality

One night while entertaining friends at Cambridge, Newton went to his room to fetch a bottle of wine and failed to return. His guests found that he had completely forgotten their presence and was hard at work at his desk.

The bubonic plague, a bacterial infection carried by a flea that infests rats, had periodically devastated Europe since the first century. England's Great Plague of 1665-1666 killed about 100,000 people.

The manor house in Woolsthorpe, Lincolnshire, where Newton was born and where he returned after leaving Cambridge in 1665. The desk in his bedroom stood before a window that overlooked an apple orchard.

THE BREAKTHROUGH

The story of an apple hitting Newton on the head as he rested under a tree, inspiring him with the theory of gravity, is the stuff of fairy tales. Good science does not come quite so easily. The famous falling apple does, however, hold a prime place in Newton's success. In fact, near the end of his life, he remembered that it was an apple that set him to thinking about a very basic question: If an apple falls to the ground, why doesn't the Moon fall to the ground?

There was clearly a force that pulled the apple to the ground. Scientists even generally referred to this force as gravity. But shouldn't this force extend into space—and eventually to the Moon? The Greek philosopher Aristotle, whose work formed the basis of traditional astronomy and physics, believed that the natural tendency of objects was to remain at rest unless acted on by some force. But Newton believed that Galileo's experiments with falling bodies proved otherwise. An object at rest might remain at rest, but an object in motion would continue to move in a straight line unless a force acted on it. This principle, called inertia, meant that if the Moon were not being acted on by some force that kept tugging it near to Earth in a curved orbit, its tendency would be to move through space in a straight line.

It was accepted that gravity came from the Earth, and Newton thought that it might logically come from the center of the Earth. He figured that an apple tree stood 4,000 miles from the central point of this force of gravity. He then calculated the rate at which the apple fell to the ground, which was approximately 16 feet per second. Newton assumed that the force of gravity was pulling the Moon toward Earth just as it pulled the apple. But he realized that if the Moon were "falling" to Earth, like the apple, at a rate of 16 feet per second, it would crash to the ground almost immediately. Something did not add up.

Newton suspected that, like other forces, gravity would become weaker the greater the distance it must cover. There was mathematical evidence that other forces became weaker at a rate that was the square of the distance of the object from the source of the force (this rule is called the inverse-square law). If the Moon was 60 times farther from the center of Earth than the apple was, then the force of gravity on the Moon would be 3,600 times weaker than the force of gravity acting on the apple (60^2=60x60=3600). If gravity followed the inverse-square law, then the Moon was falling to Earth—that is, being tugged out of straight-line motion—at a rate of 0.0044 feet per second.

Newton knew that if he threw an apple as if it were a ball, it would fall to Earth in a curve. If the Moon were also "falling" in a curve, but at a very slow speed (like 0.0044 feet per second), the curve of its fall would match the curvature of Earth's surface. That way, the Moon could "fall" forever without crashing. In other words, the same force that pulled an apple to the ground kept the Moon in its orbit.

The mathematical proofs Newton derived from this problem convinced him that he had hit upon something major: he had figured out the force that held the universe together. But geometric shapes and algebraic formulas were not sophisticated enough to represent the fluctuating properties of gravity and inertia. To calculate these interactions, mathematics had to be based, not on a point or set of points, but on a constantly moving point. To decipher the specific workings of his gravitational model, Newton used a new kind of mathematics that he had begun developing during his undergraduate studies. It was the birth of what we now know as calculus.

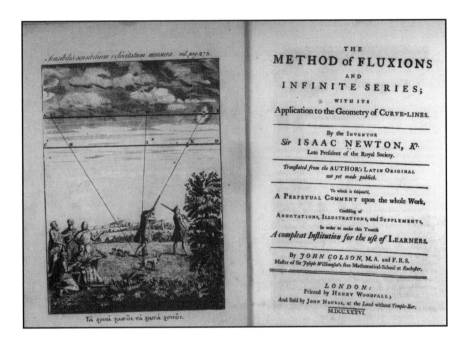

In 1667, Newton returned to Cambridge to work on his Master of Arts degree. He began doing research in optics, trying to prove his theory that white light was a combination of many different colors of light. In his work, he was constantly annoyed by the distortion of light that was caused by viewing it through a lens, as in a typical refracting telescope. When he realized that he would not be able to correct this distortion, he turned his attention to the use of a mirror instead of a lens to gather light. The product of his mechanical tinkering, built entirely from scratch, was the reflecting telescope. Not only was distortion no longer a problem, but Newton could also build a more powerful telescope in a smaller package. Efficient, effective, and cheap, the reflecting telescope became an extremely popular alternative to

Twenty-seven years passed before Newton published his invention of calculus, and even then he did so anonymously. The title page shown here is for an English translation of Newton's Latin work on the subject, published in 1736—nine years after his death. The diagram on the left shows how calculus can be used to analyze movements such as that of a hunter shooting at a bird.

Newton's reflecting telescope. Light enters the tube on the right-hand end, and a mirror at the opposite end gathers the light and reflects it to the eyepiece through which the observer looks (on the side of the tube near the right-hand end).

long, bulky refracting telescopes. Newton gained modest fame for his invention, including being admitted to the prestigious Royal Society of scientists.

In 1669, Newton was elected to the position of Lucasian Professor of Mathematics at Trinity College. But his invention of calculus and its application to the problem of gravity and the movements of the planets remained a well-guarded secret. He could not get his calculations to work perfectly—probably because he was using a slightly incorrect figure for the radius of Earth—and so he set his theories aside without publishing them. It was not until nearly 20 years later, in a conversation with his friend Edmond Halley, that Newton's secret came out.

Halley had discussed the movements of the planets with his friends from the Royal Society, scientist Robert Hooke and architect Christopher Wren. Although Johannes Kepler's laws of planetary motion were accepted as true, no one knew *why* the planets behaved as Kepler described them. But all three men felt sure that Kepler's theory of elliptical orbits could be explained if only someone could prove mathematically that gravity decreased by the square of the distance from its source. Wren even offered an expensive book as a prize to either Halley or Hooke if one of them could solve the puzzle.

When he met Newton at Cambridge several months later, Halley casually asked the mathematician what the shape of a planetary orbit would be if, in fact, gravity followed the inverse-square law.

The Royal Society's headquarters in Crane Court, London. The society was founded in 1660 by King Charles II to organize scientific discoveries and make them public. Its motto was "To improve the knowledge of natural things, and all useful Arts, Manufactures, Mechanic practices, Engines and Inventions by Experiments (not meddling with Divinity, Metaphysics, Morals, Politics, Grammar, Rhetoric or Logic)."

Edmond Halley (1656-1742) was the first major astronomer to observe the stars of the southern hemisphere. He also noticed similarities between the comets of 1531, 1607, and 1682 and theorized that these were reappearances of the same comet, orbiting the Sun in a very elongated ellipse that brought it near to Earth every 76 years. He predicted the comet would return in 1758, and although he died before seeing his prophesy come true, the comet now bears his name.

When Newton casually replied that the orbit would be elliptical, Halley was amazed. He asked how Newton knew the shape to be an ellipse, and was dumbfounded when Newton explained simply that he had calculated it and could prove it mathematically. Newton seemed unmoved, but Halley realized that what had been a massive and locked door to the universe had just been opened. He asked Newton for the calculations. After scouring through his mountains of papers without success, Newton said that he would reproduce the lost calculations and send them to Halley.

Three months later, Newton fulfilled his promise. He sent Halley a four-page paper that showed the complex mathematical proofs for Kepler's laws of planetary motion, as well as an explanation of gravitation according to the inverse-square principle. It was Halley who recognized the importance of what Newton had done and convinced him to publish his discoveries in a book. Just 18 months later, Newton had completed the 550 pages of his *Philosophiae Naturalis Principia Mathematica* (*Mathematical Principles of Natural Philosophy*), commonly known as the *Principia*.

The *Principia* followed a simple plan. The first part developed the mathematical principles that described motion, gravity, and inertia. In book two, Newton expanded on his principles to describe, for example, motion through different densities. The third section presented Newton's "System of the World," showing how his principles could be used to explain the motions of objects as changeable as the tides, as large as stars, or as small as falling apples. This was summed up in his law of universal gravitation, which stated that each object in the universe attracts every other object, and that this attractive force depends on the masses of the two objects and the distance between them. Newton developed a mathematical formula to show that objects of larger mass generate more gravitational force and that gravity becomes weaker at greater distances.

Newton then devised three laws of motion to support his proof of gravitational force. The first law is the law of inertia: an object at rest tends to stay at rest and an object in motion tends to stay in motion. The second law describes changes in inertia. It states that any change in an object's motion is related to the amount of force that causes the change and the

In contrast to present-day scientists, who often strive to make their work accessible to the general public, Newton deliberately made the *Principia* so difficult that only mathematical experts could follow his calculations. The book was so unreadable that one student commented to his friend when Newton walked by, "There goes the man that wrote a book that neither he nor anybody else understands."

mass: the amount of matter a body contains

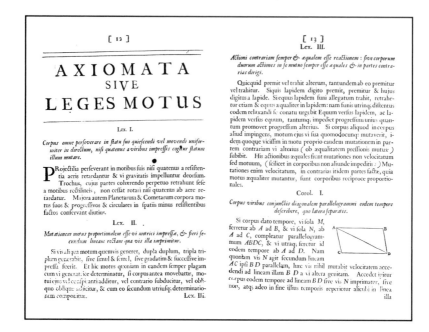

The pages of the Principia *that set forth Newton's three laws of motion*

direction from which that force strikes the object. The third law is perhaps the most famous—"To every action there is always opposed an equal reaction."

The *Principia* was published in July 1687 to widespread acclaim. Newton had offered mathematical proof of the theories of Copernicus, Kepler, and Galileo. There could be no doubt now that the universe was heliocentric, for Newton showed that large objects exert more gravitational force than smaller ones, and Earth was far too small to produce enough gravity to keep the Sun and the planets in orbit around it. Newton's work also proved that planets move in elliptical orbits because as they move away from the Sun, the force of gravity acting on them becomes weaker. To many readers, it seemed the universe had been explained at last.

THE RESULT

The fire of Newton's scientific ambition had begun to cool by the 1690s, and he spent much of the rest of his life revising his earlier works. It was a difficult time, and he apparently became bored with his life and his surroundings. He continued his work with alchemy and may even have accidentally poisoned himself during his experiments, for he suffered an emotional breakdown in 1693 that some historians attribute to chemical toxins. He longed to leave Cambridge and gladly took an administrative position as Warden of the Mint in 1696. His main duties were to supervise the minting of coins and pursue the capture of counterfeiters.

In 1701 Newton resigned his professorship, and in 1703 he was elected President of the Royal Society, which he ruled with an iron hand for 25 years. He was elected to two terms as a Member of Parliament for Cambridge University, although the only time he spoke was to ask an usher to close a drafty window. His scientific genius in these later years was devoted to his study of optics, and he published these theories of light and matter in 1704. He was knighted by Queen Anne the following year.

Newton was a man living at the highest pinnacle of fame—a living legend. But life as a legend is rarely easy, and much of the spark seemed gone from the eyes that once had been known for their intensity. On March 20, 1727, after suffering for some time from gout and inflammation of the lungs, Sir Isaac Newton, the most famous scientist England

I never knew him to take any recreation or pastime either in riding out to take the air, walking, bowling, or any other exercise whatever, thinking all hours lost that were not spent in his studies, to which he kept so close that he seldom left his chamber unless [to lecture] at term time . . . where so few went to hear him, and fewer understood him, that ofttimes he did in a manner, for want of hearers, read to the walls.
—Isaac Newton's servant

Newton—who often seemed paranoid and never took criticism well—spent much of his professional life feuding with other scientists. One of these conflicts was with Robert Hooke, who claimed that he had been the first to discover both universal gravitation and the reflecting telescope. Another was with the German mathematician Gottfried Leibniz over which man had been the first to invent calculus. Today, historians agree that Newton and Leibniz developed calculus at around the same time, independently of each other.

had ever known, died at the age of 84. He was buried in the place of ultimate honor, Westminster Abbey.

Newton did not discover anything through observation, and it could be argued that he was actually a physicist rather than an astronomer. In truth, he joined the two disciplines together forever. The science of astronomy had grown for thousands of years, but until Newton, it had been merely a gathering of pieces. Newton's gift to the scientific world was a completed puzzle—the pieces in place at last. Thanks to his mathematical proof, there were no more doubts about Kepler's laws of planetary motion or Galileo's experiments with falling objects. The world would no longer accept Aristotle's model of the universe as truth.

At the same time, however, Newton's discoveries raised as many questions as they answered. If every star and planetary body produced gravitational

Although a man of great accomplishments, Newton never married, nor did he have many close friends. Remarking on Newton's difficult personality, the writer Aldous Huxley said, "If we evolved a race of Isaac Newtons, that would not be progress. For the price Newton had to pay for being a supreme intellect was that he was incapable of friendship, love, fatherhood, and many other desirable things."

force, then there was no absolute center of the universe that remained at rest and caused all the other objects to rotate around it. The universe was infinitely complex and constantly in motion, and, as Newton himself realized, it could never be comprehended. "The orbit of any one planet," he wrote, "depends on the combined motion of all the planets, not to mention the action of all these on each other. But to consider simultaneously all these causes of motion and to define these motions by exact laws . . . exceeds, unless I am mistaken, the force of the entire human intellect." Moreover, although Newton had described the mechanics of gravity, no one knew what caused it or how one object attracted another across the vast emptiness of space—problems that remain unsolved to this day.

Nevertheless, Newton's influence on science is still felt. In 1968, when astronaut Bill Anders was asked by his son who was in control of his *Apollo 8* spacecraft, he replied, "I think Isaac Newton is doing most of the driving now." It was Newton's work that allowed scientists to calculate how much power would be needed for a rocket to escape the primary pull of Earth's gravity (escape velocity) and how fast an object must travel to remain in orbit around Earth (orbital velocity), knowledge that would help speed spacecraft on their way to the more distant reaches of our solar system—and beyond. Newton himself, however, was able to keep some perspective on his accomplishments, and to recognize those who had come before him. "If I saw farther than others," he said, "it was because I stood on the shoulders of giants."

Rehberg del.

Bollinger sc.

CHAPTER SEVEN

William Herschel and Deep Space

In the eighteenth century, some thinkers began to speculate about the nature of the universe beyond the known boundaries of our solar system. In 1755, early in his career, the philosopher Immanuel Kant correctly suggested that the stars of the Milky Way formed a disk-shaped cluster in space. From this idea, Kant went on to imagine a universe composed of many disk-shaped clusters of stars—or galaxies— like our Milky Way.

Kant then suggested that nebulae, patches of glowing material that had been observed among the stars, might actually be star systems that existed at great distances from our own galaxy. A disk-shaped galaxy viewed from varying angles, he argued, might appear round, oval, or linear—the same shapes that nebulae often had. Kant's portrait of the universe as a collection of galaxies scattered across immense gulfs of space was dramatic and fascinating. But it was the work of William Herschel that provided a

Nebula is the Latin word for "cloud" or "mist."

Frederick William Herschel (1738-1822) devoted his career to building telescopes of such size and power that he could rightfully claim, "I have looked farther into space than ever [a] human being did before me."

107

After his early studies of the galaxy, Immanuel Kant (1724-1804) went on to become an influential philosopher on such subjects as the nature of knowledge. He once called his own ideas "the Copernican revolution in philosophy."

solid foundation to support the passionate ideas of philosophers such as Kant. An amateur astronomer who became the greatest observational scientist of the late eighteenth and early nineteenth centuries, Herschel gazed beyond the known celestial objects to explore the vastness of deep space.

Friedrich Wilhelm (later anglicized as Frederick William) Herschel was born in Hanover, Germany, on November 15, 1738. He was the third of six children of Anna Ilse Moritzen and Isaac Herschel, a military musician. At the age of 15, William left school to follow in his father's footsteps, playing the oboe and violin in the same regimental band. In 1756, the regiment—along with its band, which included William, his older brother Jacob, and his father—was sent overseas to protect Germany's ally, England, against French invasion in the Seven Years' War. William quickly learned the English language and made valuable musical contacts there.

The band returned home after a few months to find battles raging and Hanover in danger of French occupation. At Isaac Herschel's encouragement, William and Jacob, neither of whom had any military training, left the band and moved to England. Jacob eventually returned to Germany, but William stayed in England, teaching, performing, conducting, and composing music. In 1766, he was offered a job as an organist for the Octagon Chapel in the fashionable resort town of Bath.

Although his position in Bath was comfortable, William Herschel hungered for new activities. His inquiring mind led him to books on astronomy, and he began to observe the night sky. In 1772, Herschel brought his younger sister Caroline to England to launch her singing career, but instead she became his assistant and a partner in his new passion for astronomical observation. Brother and sister would spend every night, even in freezing temperatures, looking at the sky and recording what they observed.

In his reading, especially of Robert Smith's book *A Compleat System of Opticks*, Herschel took to heart the notion that the larger the telescope, the deeper into space one could see. By 1773, he was so engrossed in astronomy that he was buying telescopes while building others from component parts. He began using a refracting telescope but realized, as Newton had, that it allowed chromatic aberration, or false colors, into the image. He rented a

If it had not been for the intervention of a cloudy or moonlit night I know not when he [William] or I would have got any sleep.
—Caroline Herschel

refracting telescope: a telescope in which light from an object is gathered and focused by lenses

Caroline Lucretia Herschel (1750-1848) became a well-known astronomer in her own right. She was the first woman to discover a comet. During her long career, she discovered 8 of them—not to mention 17 nebulae and many star clusters—and published a major catalog of the stars. At age 78 she was awarded the Gold Medal of the Royal Astronomical Society for her achievements, and at 96, she was given a Gold Medal for Science by the King of Prussia. A crater on the Moon bears her name.

reflecting telescope: a telescope in which light from an object is gathered and focused by a mirror

By 1789, Herschel had built 200 7-foot reflectors, 150 10-foot reflectors, and 80 20-foot reflectors.

Herschel's 7-foot reflecting telescope followed the basic design Isaac Newton had pioneered a century earlier. Herschel used this instrument for most of his early observations.

small reflecting telescope and found it to be better suited for his work.

While other astronomers of the day were pre-occupied with the study of the nearby objects of the solar system, Herschel was interested in under-standing the nature and distribution of distant stars. He realized that for such a study he would need tele-scopes with larger light-gathering ability than those he could buy or rent. Herschel diligently set out to build his own instruments. He began to cast his own mirrors out of copper and tin, grinding and polishing them to the precise concave shape required to gather and focus starlight. His workmanship with eyepieces and large mirrors was soon unequaled, and his telescope tubes were elegantly fashioned of hard-wood. After several years of building and refining,

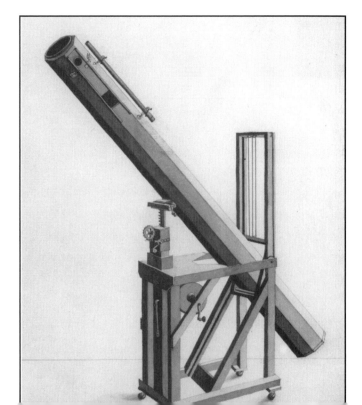

This telescope, completed in 1776, is known as Herschel's "small" 20-foot reflector. The instrument hung from a pole, and Herschel had to stand atop a tall ladder to look through the eyepiece. He improved on this design seven years later with his "large" 20-foot reflector, which was mounted on a stable framework, including a safe platform for the observer to stand on.

Herschel possessed some of the best and most powerful telescopes of his time.

Between 1779 and 1781, Herschel "swept" the heavens twice. Wearing a black hood to keep out stray light from his dark-conditioned eyes, he would move the telescope over a section of the sky. As he did so, he recorded any interesting objects. Then he would move the telescope back across on an adjacent path a little bit above or below where he began. Herschel repeated this motion up to 30 times for a "sweep." In his first sweep, he examined all of the brightest stars visible to his telescope; in his second, he discovered and cataloged 269 double and multiple stars, far more than had ever been observed before. He became so familiar with the night sky that, if something different appeared, he could distinguish it from the usual stellar landscape.

double star: two stars that appear close together in the sky. Some double stars are true **binary stars**—systems of two stars bound together by gravitational force—while others may actually lie far apart, their closeness an optical illusion.

THE BREAKTHROUGH

On the evening of March 13, 1781, while Herschel was scanning the skies for double stars, he encountered a bright object in the constellation Gemini. To his experienced eye, the object was obviously not an ordinary star. He observed it four nights later, and, finding that it had moved, supposed it was a comet. When his sighting was communicated to England's Royal Society of scientists, other astronomers began to observe the object as well. Examination of its slow orbit over the next several months revealed that this actually was a planet, twice the distance of Saturn from the Sun. The size of the known solar system had instantly doubled.

When the Royal Society asked Herschel to name the new planet, he suggested "Georgium Sidus" ("George's Star") in honor of George III, the Hanoverian king of England. The French, however, called the new planet "Herschel." Meanwhile, the German astronomer Johann Bode proposed "Uranus" as a name that would fit into the mythological theme that had already been established: Uranus was the father of Saturn, Saturn was the father of Jupiter, and Jupiter was the father of all the other gods. The new planet was called by several names until 1850, when it was recommended that Uranus become the official international name.

The discovery of Uranus was a turning point in Herschel's career. He was now famous as the first recorded discoverer of a planet. His isolation as an amateur astronomer ended. He was elected to the

Who knows what new rings, new satellites, or what other nameless and numberless phenomena remain behind [Uranus], waiting to reward future industry and improvement?
—the President of the Royal Society, on Herschel's discovery of Uranus

Royal Society and was awarded its highest honor, the Copley Medal. Herschel was even granted a royal pension that would allow him to give up his musical duties for good, and five years later the king gave Caroline a similar income for her own scientific contributions. The siblings moved near the royal residence of Windsor Castle, eventually settling in Slough at an estate known as Observatory House. Herschel manufactured and sold telescopes to supplement his pension. Although not wealthy, he was free from severe financial strain and could devote all his time to astronomy.

Herschel now set out to build an even larger telescope than any he had built before. Several attempts to cast a three-foot-wide mirror in his basement ended in disaster; in one memorable episode, the mold for the mirror cracked and Caroline and William had to run for their lives from flowing molten metal. In 1785, however, Herschel received a grant from the king for another attempt at a large instrument. After four years of labor under Herschel's direction, a team of workmen completed the largest reflecting telescope in the world. Using this 40-foot-long instrument, Herschel almost immediately discovered the sixth and seventh satellites of Saturn, Enceladus and Mimas. But the telescope was never fully satisfactory for everyday use. The one-ton, four-foot mirror warped, misted, and tarnished easily. Worse yet, the instrument was cumbersome to position; Herschel had to stand atop a 50-foot-high scaffold to look into it, while shouting instructions down to a team of laborers who aimed the scope at a

Oliver Wendell Holmes, an American doctor and writer, described Herschel's 40-foot telescope as "a mighty bewilderment of slanted masts, spars and ladders and ropes, from the midst of which a vast tube . . . lifted its mighty muzzle defiantly towards the sky."

particular section of the sky. Although the huge telescope impressed Herschel's visitors, he preferred to make most of his observations with smaller instruments, such as the one he used to discover Uranus.

Herschel's personal life had taken a back seat to his obsession with astronomy, but in 1788—at nearly 50 years of age—he married his neighbor's widow, Mary Pitt. William and Mary's only son, John Frederick, was born in 1792 and began assisting his father and aunt with their observations as soon as he was old enough.

William Herschel continued to review the sky, studying not only the stars, but also a number of objects within the solar system. He discovered two satellites of Uranus and determined that they move in retrograde (reverse), observed sunspots and the rings of Saturn, and studied the polar ice caps of Mars. His attention, however, always returned to the stars beyond. So much had yet to be learned about their number, origin, locations, and distances from Earth, and Herschel knew that his powerful telescopes could penetrate some of their mysteries.

Between 1781 and 1802, Herschel identified 2,500 deep space nebulae. Able to bring greater resolution to these cloudy patches than any astronomer had before, he discovered that the nebulae he observed were actually clusters of distant stars. He therefore assumed that all nebulae were star clusters, and if individual stars could not be detected in a specific nebula, it must be because of the great distance. With more powerful telescopes, Herschel decided, all nebulae could be resolved into star clusters.

From his observations, Herschel knew that stars could exert gravitational force on one another; in fact, binary stars moved in orbits around each other. He concluded that the same force of universal gravitation forms stars into clusters. Herschel theorized that the Sun belongs to one of these vast clusters of stars, and he even tried to map it. His diagram of the galaxy was based on false assumptions (he believed that all stars have the same brightness, so stars that appear brighter to viewers on Earth must be closer than dim stars) and was not accurate.

In 1802, Herschel carefully observed Ceres and Pallas, celestial bodies between Mars and Jupiter. Calculating their diameters to be under 200 miles and detecting their difference from other planets and comets, he suggested a new term: "asteroid." He proceeded to forecast that more such bodies would be discovered, and, of course, they were. About 20,000 asteroids have been observed, most of them located in the "asteroid belt" between Mars and Jupiter.

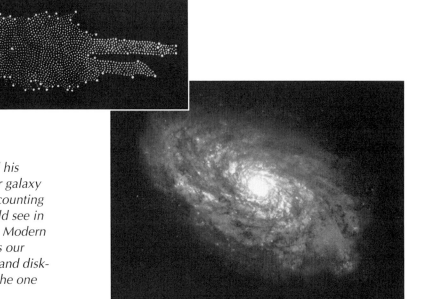

Herschel produced his cross-section of our galaxy (above) by simply counting all the stars he could see in various directions. Modern photography shows our galaxy to be spiral and disk-shaped, similar to the one pictured at right.

It was, however, the first attempt of its kind, and it was frequently reproduced in books throughout the nineteenth century. Furthermore, Herschel was correct in realizing that we see the Milky Way—a band of brightness in the night sky—because Earth is situated within the layer of stars that forms our galaxy (which is sometimes called the Milky Way galaxy).

Then, on November 13, 1790, Herschel's theories were challenged when he observed a nebula in the constellation of Taurus that was not a cluster of stars at all, but a central star with a luminous shell around it. He decided that this nebula was a young star that was still in the process of condensing from the cloud of dust and gases that surrounded it. Modifying his earlier hypothesis, Herschel declared that what appeared to viewers on Earth as nebulae were really stars in different stages of formation. Nebulous clouds gradually condensed into individual stars, which then gradually condensed into clusters of stars. Eventually, these clusters would grow so dense that they collapsed, becoming clouds of debris that would someday re-form into new stars. More fascinated by the variety of the heavens than bothered by having been wrong in some of his earlier theories, Herschel had become the first scientist to collect evidence of the natural history of the universe.

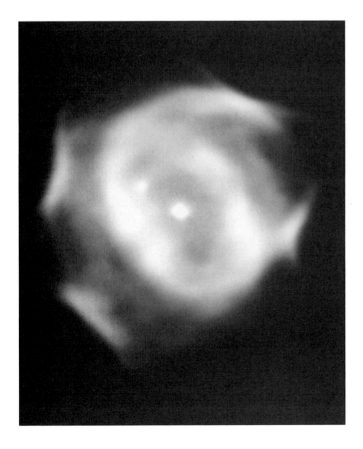

Planetary nebulae—such as the one Herschel observed in November 1790 and the one shown here—are actually not new, developing stars but old, unstable ones that have emitted a glowing cloud of gas. Nevertheless, Herschel's conclusions about how stars evolve were valid enough to lay the foundation for further study by astronomers of the nineteenth and twentieth centuries.

THE RESULT

Ironically, much of Herschel's work was not immediately accepted because it was simply too good. When other astronomers looked at the sky with their less powerful, often distorting telescopes, they saw none of the wonders that Herschel described. He was not even a trained astronomer, and yet if his discoveries were true, their potential was revolutionary. Not only had his sighting of Uranus expanded the size of the known solar system, but he had also shown that the universe extends far beyond that boundary. By locating the solar system within a galaxy and then finding thousands of similar galaxies unimaginable distances away, he suggested that Earth and its Sun were just a tiny part of the vast universe.

Herschel's theories about the way that stars formed and collapsed created a portrait of a universe that was constantly evolving. His ideas were the natural extension of Isaac Newton's law of universal gravitation, for Herschel detailed the ways that stellar debris was drawn together to form stars and stars were drawn together to form galaxies. Herschel even discovered that the Sun itself was moving, influenced by the gravitational pull of other stars and planets. The universe, he demonstrated, had not remained constant since the beginning of time. It was not contained and stable, as the models of Claudius Ptolemy or Nicolaus Copernicus had been, but huge, changing, and still largely unknown.

Even in his seventies and eighties, Herschel continued to watch the skies and refine his theories,

In 1718, Edmond Halley had discovered that some stars had moved from the positions in which they were observed by ancient astronomers.

John Frederick Herschel (1792-1871) continued and perfected his father's work with stars and nebulae. Elected to the Royal Society at just 21 years of age, he rose to become one of the most famous British scientists of his day. Using one of his father's 20-foot reflectors, he produced the first detailed survey of the stars south of the equator, thereby becoming the first astronomer in history to examine the entire sky systematically with a major telescope.

despite the fact that he had become very ill in 1808 and never fully recovered his health. In 1816, his son, John, returned home from Cambridge to serve as his father's assistant. In that same year, William Herschel was knighted in recognition of his great achievements. He was still at work when he died at his home in Slough on August 25, 1822, at the age of 84. The epitaph on his grave was *Coelorum perrupit claustra*— "He broke through the barriers of the heavens."

A knowledge of the construction of the heavens has always been the ultimate object of my observation.
—William Herschel

In some ways, the musician and amateur stargazer had been out of step with the science of his time. While other astronomers used the tight focus of refracting telescopes to observe the planets, Herschel was capturing the light of distant nebulae with his huge reflectors. While other astronomers calculated the positions of the known bodies within the solar system and predicted their movements, Herschel was looking deep into the past of intergalactic space, at stars whose light had taken millions of years to reach Earth.

And yet, Herschel's work represented the future of astronomy. Throughout the next two centuries, scientists strove to build ever-larger telescopes that would penetrate even deeper into space. In Ireland in 1845, William Parsons, the Third Earl of Rosse, used his considerable wealth to build a 72-foot-long reflector with which he determined the spiral nature of a distant nebula. In the early twentieth century, the American astronomer George Ellery Hale campaigned for the construction of two successive reflectors—the Mount Wilson and Mount Palomar telescopes—each in turn the largest in the world for its time and both still in use today. Hale's telescope at Williams Bay, Wisconsin, remains the world's largest operating refracting telescope.

In the late 1970s, scientists began developing telescopes that would truly break through the barriers of the heavens—instruments that would operate in space, outside Earth's distorting atmosphere. Their efforts culminated in the Hubble Space Telescope, which was launched into orbit around

Earth in April 1990. The Hubble has captured such spectacular images of deep space that it has been called "the new window on the universe," fulfilling the goal that William Herschel strove toward nearly 200 years before as he swept the skies with his remarkable telescopes.

William Parsons's 72-foot reflector had two 6-foot mirrors that weighed four tons apiece—the largest mirrors that had ever been cast.

Beyond the Stars

In December 1993, a National Aeronautics and Space Administration (NASA) crew blasted off from Kennedy Space Center aboard the space shuttle *Endeavour*. As they headed toward a rendezvous with the Hubble Space Telescope (HST) 370 miles above the Earth, the future of astronomy seemed to be resting on their shoulders.

NASA had launched the HST into orbit around Earth more than three years earlier. The massive project was the result of over a decade of research and planning. Despite its potential for shaping the future of astronomy, however, the HST was also a reflection of astronomy's past. In 1609, Galileo Galilei had been one of the first to turn a telescope to the heavens. In 1668, Isaac Newton had developed the reflecting telescope, providing the basic design for the HST. At the turn of the nineteenth century, William Herschel had striven to build ever-larger and more advanced telescopes to

The Hubble Space Telescope represents a new era of technology in the age-old science of astronomy.

see farther into deep space. And so things had continued, step by step, into the late twentieth century.

The Hubble Space Telescope promised to be more than just another step into increasingly distant reaches of space. With its location outside Earth's atmosphere, it had the power to push the boundaries of our vision so far into the distance that some astronomers considered the possibility of seeing to the very edge of the universe.

And then came the disappointment.

The 96-inch primary mirror in the HST, the smoothest mirror ever used in a large astronomical instrument, had been ground to the wrong shape. Although the flaw was less than the width of a hair, it was enough to blur the images that the telescope received. The HST seemed to be, as more than one astronomer noted, the biggest catastrophe in the history of telescopes.

And so, in 1993, the crew of the *Endeavour* held the hopes of the entire astronomical community as they docked with the HST and installed "corrective lenses" to neutralize the mirror's flaw. They spent many hours of exhausting work in space, tethered to their shuttle as they worked on the telescope.

The mission was a dramatic success, and in fact the telescope soon exceeded expectations. Just one month after the completion of the HST repairs, dramatic, beautifully detailed images were radioed to Earth of the comet Shoemaker-Levy 9 as it broke apart and smashed into Jupiter. Other images followed, from our neighboring planets to the most distant points in the universe. The HST has studied

Astronauts Jeffrey A. Hoffman (right) and F. Story Musgrave finish installing a new camera (the white rectangle on the lower part of the telescope) on the HST during the 1993 repair mission.

the surface of Pluto, confirmed the existence of black holes, helped define the rate at which the universe is expanding, and—as its creators had hoped—allowed astronomers to see more of the universe (and more clearly) than ever before.

The Hubble Space Telescope is only one example of the ways in which modern astronomers have built upon the work of earlier thinkers to see—either literally or theoretically—farther out into the

In its first 10 years of operation, the HST orbited Earth 58,400 times, observed 14,000 different celestial targets, and generated 3.5 terabytes (3.5 trillion bytes) of data.

universe. After William Herschel discovered Uranus in 1781, astronomers charting the planet's orbit found that it kept drifting from its path. Based on Newton's theory of universal gravitation, scientists suspected that Uranus's orbit was being affected by the gravitational pull of some nearby celestial body. Sure enough, in 1846 Johann Galle discovered that beyond Uranus lay another planet, which became known as Neptune. In 1930, Clyde Tombaugh discovered Pluto beyond Neptune. Astronomers had gone even further by the year 2000: they had located about 50 planets orbiting sun-like stars beyond the boundaries of our solar system! Although these planets cannot be seen from Earth, scientists can detect the minute wobble of a star as it is tugged by the gravity of a planet that orbits it.

While today's astronomers no longer puzzle about the structure of the solar system—as Claudius Ptolemy, Nicolaus Copernicus, and Tycho Brahe did centuries before—their work expands upon the quest begun by these early thinkers. In 1989, for instance, Margaret Geller and John Huchra managed to make a three-dimensional map of a small "slice" of the universe. The map showed galaxies arranged in a structure that resembled a stick figure. When Geller and Huchra expanded their map to adjacent parts of the universe, they found that a band of galaxies stretched horizontally across the center in a formation that is now called the Great Wall. Discovering that galaxies form patterns—the largest known patterns in nature—helped Geller feel connected to the scientists who came before her. "We learn in school that Ptolemy was this idiot who thought the Earth was the center of the universe," she said. "In my opinion that was a minor idea of Ptolemy's compared to the idea that maps are useful as scale representations of physical systems; that idea underlies much of modern science. Today, we map the human genome. We make a map of the arrangement of atoms in molecules. . . . We map the distribution of species in the rain forest. We map the universe."

Margaret Geller holding her "stick figure" map of a slice of the universe

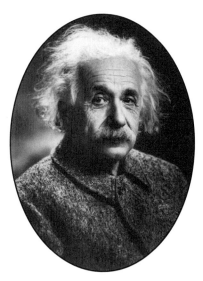

Albert Einstein (1879-1955) is one of the most famous scientists in history. Not only did he revolutionize physics with his theories about space, time, and gravity, but he was also a champion of world peace.

To understand the way a celestial object of large mass could curve space and cause smaller bodies to be attracted to it, imagine a bowling ball sitting on a waterbed. The mattress would curve beneath the weight of the ball. If you were to drop a marble onto the mattress, it would roll toward the bowling ball.

Like Johannes Kepler and Isaac Newton, modern astronomers also strive to understand how the universe works. Between 1905 and 1916, Albert Einstein published his theories of relativity, which radically redefined how scientists think about bodies moving in space. Einstein suggested the universe is not three-dimensional, but four-dimensional—that it not only includes space, but also time, so that looking at the stars means looking back in time as well as out into space. Space and time, he proposed, are not constant; they change depending on how fast and in what direction we are moving as we perceive them. Einstein also theorized that gravity is an effect caused by the fact that space is curved. Celestial bodies of large mass, such as planets, create curves in space that cause smaller bodies, such as moons, to fall toward them. Today, astrophysicist Stephen Hawking (who holds the same honorary position at Cambridge University once held by Isaac Newton) builds on Einstein's theories to explore mysteries early astronomers might never have dreamed of, such as the behavior of black holes, the expansion of the universe, and even the origin of space and time.

Although the questions asked by astronomers may have changed over time, their goals have remained the same. Today's scientists still seek theories that explain their observations, and they still fight established beliefs when observable data contradict them. Astronomy has become much more complex and technologically advanced, spreading into more areas of science than ever before, but the pattern remains: each new watcher of the skies

Stephen Hawking (b. 1942) poses beneath a portrait of Sir Isaac Newton. Since the 1960s, Hawking has suffered from ALS (also called Lou Gehrig's disease), a fatal disease that affects the central nervous system. He uses a wheelchair and communicates with the aid of a computer. In addition to his work in quantum physics, he has published popular books for non-scientists, including A Brief History of Time.

stands upon the shoulders of those who came before. As astronomy has evolved, humanity's view of our planet, our universe, and our place in the cosmic order has been transformed. But despite the advances that have been made, the extent of our knowledge is dwarfed by the number of things we have yet to understand. And so people all over the world still gaze up at the night sky, peering through their telescopes in the hopes of finding something new. Their quest is evidence of the one truth of astronomy that has, for thousands of years, kept it exciting and growing and ever-new: there is always a place in astronomy for discovery.

GLOSSARY

alchemy: an early form of chemistry with philosophical and magical associations; alchemists sought to change base metals into gold and give human beings immortality

asteroid: a small rocky or metallic body, also known as a minor planet, that orbits the Sun and shines by reflected light

astrology: the study of the positions of the Sun, Moon, stars, and planets in the belief that they influence earthly events and human fortunes

astronomy: the science that studies the stars, planets, and all other celestial bodies

binary star: a system of two stars bound together by gravitational force; *see also* **double star**

calculus: the branch of mathematics that deals with continuously changing quantities

celestial: relating to the sky or the heavens. Aristotle believed that the celestial realm was perfect and unchanging.

celestial equator: the space above Earth's equator

comet: a body made up of dust and ice that moves among the planets. When a comet passes near the Sun, the heat creates a glowing tail of vapor that is often visible from Earth.

conjunction: the apparent alignment of two or more celestial bodies

double star: two stars that appear close together in the sky. Some double stars are true **binary stars**, while others may actually lie far apart, their closeness an optical illusion.

eccentric: in Ptolemaic theory, the displacement of Earth from the exact center of the universe

eclipse: the passage of one celestial body through the shadow of another. In a **solar eclipse**, the Moon blocks the light from the Sun to Earth; in a **lunar eclipse**, Earth blocks the light of the Sun to the Moon.

ellipse: an oval-shaped figure with two centers of symmetry, called **foci** (plural of focus). The orbits of planets are elliptical.

epicycle: in Ptolemaic theory, a circular orbit whose center moves along the circumference of another, larger, circle

equant: in Ptolemaic theory, an imaginary center point—the "mirror image" of Earth's position—around which the planets revolve

equinox: either of the two times of the year—in spring and autumn—when the Sun crosses the celestial equator, making day and night of equal length in all parts of the Earth. The vernal (spring) equinox is around March 21 and the autumnal (fall) equinox is around September 23.

galaxy: a large grouping of stars bound together by gravitational force into one of three major shapes—spiral, elliptical, or irregular. Earth and its solar system are located in a spiral galaxy referred to as the Galaxy, sometimes called the Milky Way galaxy.

geocentric: the model that depicts Earth as the unmoving center of the solar system

gravity: universal, mutual attraction of all objects for one another; the force that tends to draw all bodies within Earth's atmosphere toward the center of the Earth

heliocentric: the model in which the Sun is at the center of the solar system

inertia: the tendency of every body at rest to remain at rest and every body in motion to remain in motion, unless acted upon by a force

magnitude: a measure of the brightness of a star or other celestial object, expressed on a scale in which the lowest numbers indicate the greatest brightness

mass: the amount of matter a body contains

Milky Way: a softly glowing band of light visible in the sky from Earth, produced by the stars and nebulae that make up the galaxy in which Earth and its solar system are located. This galaxy is often called the Milky Way galaxy.

nebula (plural **nebulae**): the general term for a vast, diffuse, celestial object visible in the night sky. Planetary nebulae are shells of gas from old, unstable stars; reflection or emission nebulae are clouds of dust and gas that glow from the light of nearby stars; elliptical or spiral nebulae are other galaxies, viewed at a great distance.

observatory: a place designed and equipped for making observations of astronomical, meteorological, or other natural phenomena

optics: the branch of physics that deals with light and its interaction with matter

orbit: the movement of one celestial body around another, under the influence of gravitational force

physics: the science that studies the interactions of matter and energy, and attempts to describe them in terms of simple laws

planet: a major celestial body that orbits the Sun or another star; there are nine known planets in Earth's solar system

polyhedron: a solid figure, such as a cube, that is made up of polygons (flat shapes made of straight lines, like a square). The five perfect polyhedrons, also called Platonic solids, are: tetrahedron, cube, octahedron, dodecahedron, and icosahedron.

precession of the equinoxes: the 25,800-year cycle in which the equinox occurs slightly earlier each year, due to the slow wobbling of Earth on its axis

reflecting telescope: a telescope in which light from an object is gathered and focused by a mirror

refracting telescope: a telescope in which light from an object is gathered and focused by lenses

retrograde: the brief, regularly occurring, apparently backward movement of a planet in its orbit when seen from Earth, an illusion caused by the motion of the Earth at a different speed than that of the planet observed. (Some bodies, however, such as the moons of Uranus, actually do move in retrograde, orbiting in a direction opposite to that of the planets.)

satellite: a smaller celestial body that orbits a larger one (usually a planet, in which case it is also called a moon). An artificial satellite is an unmanned space vehicle designed to orbit a larger body, usually Earth.

sextant: an instrument used to measure the angles and distances of celestial bodies from each other or from the horizon

solar system: the Sun and the bodies that orbit it, including the planets and their satellites, plus asteroids, comets, and meteors

solstice: either of the two times of the year—in summer and winter—when the Sun is farthest away from the celestial equator. In the Northern Hemisphere, the summer solstice is the longest day of the year and the winter solstice is the shortest.

star: a large, gaseous celestial body held together by its own gravity that radiates light and other energy from nuclear reactions in its core; visible from Earth as a stationary, twinkling point of light

supernova: an exploding star

terrestrial: relating to Earth or its inhabitants. Aristotle believed that, in contrast to the heavens, the terrestrial realm was imperfect and always changing.

universe: everything that exists as matter—including the solar system, the galaxies, and intergalactic space—regarded as a whole

BIBLIOGRAPHY

Armitage, Angus. *William Herschel*. London: Thomas Nelson & Sons, 1962.

"Astronomers Discover 10 More Orbiting Planets." Minneapolis *Star Tribune*, August 6, 2000.

Beatty, J. Kelly, and Andrew Chaikin. *The New Solar System*. Cambridge, Mass.: Sky Publishing, 1990.

Cajori, Florian, trans. *Sir Isaac Newton's Mathematical Principles*. Berkeley: University of California Press, 1992.

Clawson, Calvin C. *Mathematical Mysteries: The Beauty and Magic of Numbers*. New York: Plenum Press, 1996.

Dobrzycki, Jerzy, ed. *The Reception of Copernicus's Heliocentric Theory*. Boston: D. Reidel, 1973.

Donahue, William H., trans. *Johannes Kepler: New Astronomy*. Cambridge: Cambridge University Press, 1992.

Dreyer, J. L. E. *Tycho Brahe: A Picture of Scientific Life and Work in the Sixteenth Century*. Edinburgh: Adam and Charles Black, 1890.

Fahie, J. J. *Galileo: His Life and Work*. London: John Murray, 1903.

Feldman, Anthony and Peter Ford. *Scientists & Inventors*. New York: Facts on File, 1979.

Ferris, Timothy. *Coming of Age in the Milky Way*. New York: William Morrow, 1988.

————. *The Whole Shebang: A State-of-the-Universe(s) Report*. New York: Simon & Schuster, 1997.

Gillispie, Charles Coulston. *Dictionary of Scientific Biography*. New York: Charles Scribner's Sons, 1970.

Gingerich, Owen. *The Eye of Heaven: Ptolemy, Copernicus, Kepler.* New York: American Institute of Physics, 1993.

Halpern, Paul. *Cosmic Wormholes: The Search for Interstellar Shortcuts.* New York: Dutton, 1992.

Hathaway, Nancy. *The Friendly Guide to the Universe.* New York: Viking, 1994.

Hawking, Stephen. *A Brief History of Time: From the Big Bang to Black Holes.* New York: Bantam, 1988.

Horgan, John. *The End of Science: Facing the Limits of Knowledge in the Twilight of the Scientific Age.* Reading, Mass.: Addison-Wesley, 1996.

Hoskin, Michael. *William Herschel and the Construction of the Heavens.* New York: Norton, 1964.

————, ed. *The Cambridge Illustrated History of Astronomy.* Cambridge: Cambridge University Press, 1997.

Hoyle, Fred. *Astronomy.* Garden City, N.Y.: Doubleday, 1962.

Levy, David H. *The Ultimate Universe.* New York: Simon & Schuster, 1998.

Menzel, Donald H. *Astronomy.* New York: Random House, 1975.

Neal, Valerie, Cathleen S. Lewis, and Frank H. Winter. *Spaceflight: A Smithsonian Guide.* New York: Macmillan, 1995.

Nicholson, Iain, and Patrick Moore. *The Universe.* New York: Macmillan, 1985.

Panek, Richard. *Seeing and Believing: How the Telescope Opened Our Eyes and Minds to the Heavens.* New York: Viking, 1998.

Pannekoek, A. *A History of Astronomy.* London: George Allen & Unwin, 1961.

Penne, Bill. *The Illustrated Guide to Astronomy.* Secaucus, N.J.: Chartwell, 1993.

Rees, Martin. *Before the Beginning: Our Universe and Others.* Reading, Mass.: Addison-Wesley, 1997.

Reston, James, Jr. *Galileo: A Life.* New York: HarperCollins, 1994.

Ronan, Colin. *The Astronomers.* New York: Hill and Wang, 1964.

Sagan, Carl. *Billions and Billions.* New York: Random House, 1997.

———. *Cosmos.* New York: Random House, 1980.

Silverberg, Robert. *Four Men Who Changed the Universe.* New York: G. P. Putnam's Sons, 1968.

Space Telescope Science Institute. "Hubblesite." hubble.stsci.edu, cited August 18, 2000.

Voelkel, James R. *Johannes Kepler and the New Astronomy.* Oxford: Oxford University Press, 1999.

White, Michael. *Isaac Newton: The Last Sorcerer.* Reading, Mass.: Perseus, 1997.

Wills, Steven R. *Mind-Boggling Astronomy.* Petersborough, N.H.: Cobblestone, 1995.

INDEX

ABOUT THE AUTHORS

Susan and Steven Wills are both educators and writers. Steven, a teacher for the last 30 years, is also the author of *Mind-Boggling Astronomy* and writes frequently for science magazines. His weekly newspaper education column has been syndicated since 1984. Susan, with over 20 years of classroom experience, is the author of science articles for more than a dozen children's and young adult magazines. Susan and Steven live and work near Philadelphia, Pennsylvania.

PHOTO ACKNOWLEDGMENTS

Archive Photos: pp. 16, 17, 20, 85, 86
Bettmann/Corbis: pp. 64, 72
English Heritage Photo Library/Kim Williams: p. 9
Harvard-Smithsonian Center for Astrophysics: p. 127
Hulton Getty/Archive Photos: pp. 10, 51, 57, 88
Library of Congress: cover (left), pp. 2, 6, 11, 14, 19, 27, 28, 30, 33, 38, 41, 42, 44, 49, 50, 54, 58, 69, 74, 87, 89, 90, 97, 100, 102, 104, 106, 108, 109, 119, 128, back cover
NASA: pp. 116 (right), 117, 122, 125
Paul Almasy/Corbis: p. 35

Reuters/Martin Langfield/Archive Photos: p. 129
Revilo: pp. 32, 59, 66, 84
Royal Astronomical Society Library: pp. 110, 111
The Royal Society: pp. 94, 98, 99
Yerkes Observatory: cover (center), pp. 12, 18, 36, 52, 53, 60, 80, 81, 82, 83, 114, 116 (left), 121